THE 🦉 LINCOLN LIBRARY *of*

GREEK & ROMAN MYTHOLOGY

VOLUME 1 ABYLA TO ATALANTA

Editors
Timothy and Susan Gall

Contributing Editor
Rick M. Newton, Ph.D., Professor of Classics, Kent State University

The Lincoln Library Press, Cleveland, Ohio

The Lincoln Library of Greek & Roman Mythology

For more information contact: The Lincoln Library Press, 812 Huron Road E Ste 401, Cleveland, Ohio 44115–1172. Or visit our web site at: www.TheLincolnLibrary.com

The Lincoln Library Press is an imprint of, and The Lincoln Library owl is a trademark of, Eastword Publications Development, Inc., Cleveland, Ohio.

Although every effort has been made to ensure the accuracy of the information contained herein, The Lincoln Library Press does not guarantee the accuracy of the data. Errors submitted to and verified by the publisher will be corrected in future editions.

Library of Congress Control Number: 2005935020

ISBN-13: 978-0-912168-21-0

ISBN-10: 0-912168-21-8 (set)

The Lincoln Library Press,
dedicated to inspiring independent learning,
is named for Abraham Lincoln,
America's foremost autodidact.

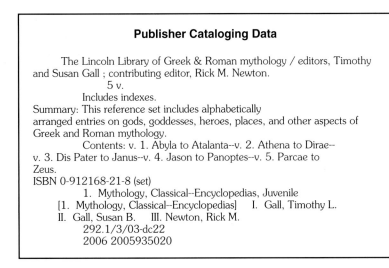

Publisher Cataloging Data

The Lincoln Library of Greek & Roman mythology / editors, Timothy and Susan Gall ; contributing editor, Rick M. Newton.
5 v.
Includes indexes.
Summary: This reference set includes alphabetically arranged entries on gods, goddesses, heroes, places, and other aspects of Greek and Roman mythology.
Contents: v. 1. Abyla to Atalanta--v. 2. Athena to Dirae--v. 3. Dis Pater to Janus--v. 4. Jason to Panoptes--v. 5. Parcae to Zeus.
ISBN 0-912168-21-8 (set)
1. Mythology, Classical--Encyclopedias, Juvenile
[1. Mythology, Classical--Encyclopedias] I. Gall, Timothy L.
II. Gall, Susan B.   III. Newton, Rick M.
292.1/3/03-dc22
2006 2005935020

Manufactured in Hong Kong

10 9 8 7 6 5 4 3 2 1

CONTENTS

Volume 1

We are all Greeks. Our laws, our literature, our religion, our arts have their roots in Greece.

Thus writes English poet Percy Bysshe Shelley (1792–1822) in his *Preface to Hellas.* Three things are amazing about this declaration. First, it was written not by a Greek but by an Englishman. If a Greek poet were to expound on the greatness of Greek culture, we might dismiss the boast as an expression of ethnocentric pride or even chauvinism. But the fact that an English poet can state "We are all Greeks" suggests that Shelley found something in the Greeks that transcends cultural boundaries and unites educated people.

Second, Shelley wrote in the early nineteenth century, some 2,500 years after the creation of Homer's *Iliad* and *Odyssey*, and some 2,300 years after the Golden Age of Periclean Athens. Shelley apparently found something in the Greeks that transcends time. For him, the ancients were as vibrant and relevant in his own day as they were in antiquity.

Third, Shelley's statement was written some 200 years before

A photograph of the Parthenon in Athens, Greece, as it appeared in the late 1800s.

the era in which we now live. As we embark on the twenty-first century, we find that his assessment still holds true. In schools, colleges, and universities throughout England, the United States, Europe, Australia, and elsewhere, the "classical curriculum" rooted in Greek culture still provides the backbone of humanistic education and the liberal arts. This suggests that there is something in Greek culture that is of permanent and eternal relevance. Just as the ancients were alive for Shelley, so is his assessment still alive for us. Even today, we are "all Greeks"!

Greece Has Taken Us Captive

But Shelley was not the first to recognize the lasting universal value of the Greeks, whose culture expressed itself in the language of mythology, gods, and heroes. As early as the second century B.C., when Rome conquered Greece and reduced her status to that of a province, the mighty conqueror confessed, "We have conquered Greece, but Greece has taken us captive through her culture." Thus wrote Roman poet Horace in *Epistles* II.1 in the first century B.C.

When the Romans turned their attention to arts, literature, and religion, they found their inspira-

tion in the very Greeks they had overcome. The first work of Latin literature was written around 273 B.C. by Livius Andronicus: a Latin translation of Homer's *Odyssey* for school children. This text not only translated Homer but, more importantly, adapted him for a young Roman audience. Thus began the classical tradition of calling the Greek "Hermes" by the Latin name of "Mercury," and of naming the Greek "Muses" as "Camenae." This tradition was honored by the epic poet Vergil, whose *Aeneid* traced the greatness of Rome to her origins in the tales first told by Homer. The Romans were proud to call themselves Romans, but they knew full well that their cultural origins lay in Greece. Expressed most simply, the Romans—like Shelley—saw themselves when they looked to Greece.

A Rebirth of High Culture

Thus was born the "Greco-Roman Civilization" which, centuries after Rome's fall, was rediscovered in the Italian and European Renaissance. As Europe awoke from the Dark Ages and found her "rebirth" in the high culture of the Greeks and Romans, she created the modern "Arts and Sciences" and gave them all classical names: poetry, drama, theater, tragedy, comedy, history, philosophy, theology, psychology,

Preface (continued)

rhetoric, biology, chemistry, architecture, mathematics, geometry, geography, astronomy, technology, anatomy, medicine, physics, politics, government, and democracy are all words of Greek and Latin origin. In short, we find the "life of the mind" when we turn to the Greeks and Romans.

A Permanent Part of Our Modern Life and Culture

Even today, as we explore outer space, investigate science, advance in technology, and pursue the arts, we "translate" our discoveries into Greek and Roman mythical terms that enable us to recognize and understand them. From the rings of Saturn to the Polyphemus moth, from the *Titanic* to the NASA Daedalus Project, from narcissism to the Oedipus complex, from our Achilles' heel to our Achilles' tendon, and even down to the trade names of Ajax cleanser and breakfast *cereals* (sacred to Ceres, goddess of grain), the myths of the Greeks and Romans have become an integral and permanent part of our modern life and culture.

The founding fathers of the United States were themselves educated in the classical tradition and, for this reason, designed the cultural and political life of the New World according to the Greco-Roman model. The American work-ethic and pioneer spirit can be traced back to the Romans, who saw themselves as pious, hard-working farmers as well as tough soldiers who boldly crossed the mountains of the Alps and the Mediterranean Sea to spread their sphere of influence. But the culture they spread was also a Hellenized culture rooted in the arts and spirit of the Greeks. One need only take a cursory glance at the public buildings in every American city—with their Greek marble columns and Roman domes—to recognize the "neoclassical" models of our civic architecture.

The classical influence extends even to the inner portions of these structures. The hallways of the Library of Congress in Washington, D.C., are a veritable treasure-trove of colorful frescoes depicting myths and legends from the Greco-Roman past, reminding us that the very notions of public "library" and "museum" are inventions of the ancients that still enrich our lives.

An Essential Component in Education

The Lincoln Library of Greek & Roman Mythology is offered to young readers in the belief that the cultural legacy of the Greco-Roman classics, as told in their fascinating myths, remains—even in the twenty-first century—an essential component in education.

The myths in this five-volume set are told in an easily readable and engaging story-like style that promises to captivate youthful enthusiasm and curiosity. At the same time, however, the texts do not "speak down" to the young. On the contrary, students are encouraged to stretch their minds and imaginations as they reflect on these stories and learn about their continuing legacy in art, science, and history.

Richly illustrated and cross-referenced, *The Lincoln Library of Greek & Roman Mythology* is designed to entice the reader to continue exploring the connections and ramifications of these marvelously intertwined tales of gods and heroes.

Rick M. Newton, Ph.D.
Professor of Classics
Kent State University

READER'S GUIDE

The Lincoln Library of Greek & Roman Mythology is designed for use by students in grades four through twelve. Organized in five volumes and arranged A to Z, *The Lincoln Library of Greek & Roman Mythology* presents entries on 500 gods, goddesses, heroes, places, and other aspects of Greek and Roman mythology.

Greek and Roman Gods

The Lincoln Library of Greek & Roman Mythology presents separate entries on the Greek and Roman gods and heroes. The first myths were created by the ancient Greeks. The Greek gods and heroes, with their attributes and myths, are presented in *The Lincoln Library of Greek & Roman Mythology* in complete entries. The Romans later adopted many of the Greek deities, but renamed them and, in some cases, recast their stories to emphasize Roman values and ideas. *The Lincoln Library of Greek & Roman Mythology* presents the Roman versions of the myths in full entries as well. Thus, both Heracles, the Greek hero, and Hercules, his Roman counterpart, have their own entries. The stories may be similar, but our editors have taken care to include only Greek character names in the Greek versions and only Roman character names in the Roman versions. The entries for some of the gods, where the myths and attributes were identical for the Greek and Roman characters, have some redundancy. The editors were committed to eliminating as much confusion for the student researcher as possible.

Features

Each entry begins with the title. If the subject is Greek, the spelling of the name in Greek follows the heading. The pronunciation guide encourages readers to say long Greek and Roman names out loud, and supports classroom presentations. The character is identified as Greek or Roman, and the attributes by which he or she is known are listed.

A brief abstract opens the longer entries, summarizing the key aspects of the character's life and/or role in mythology.

The entry text follows. Longer entries include features to draw the reader into the text, such as subheads and True/False anticipation guides. Designed with the advice of Dr. Mary Spor, an expert on reading in the content areas, these True/False statements encourage the reader to delve into the text to distinguish the true from the false.

More than 400 illustrations accompany the entries. Images filling the pages of each volume include Greco-Roman sculpture, vase-paintings, and statues; great works of Renaissance and modern art; graphics of the constellations and photographs from the exploration of outer space; comic-style panels; and photographs of plants, insects, and animals whose names were inspired by mythology. The illustrations were selected to satisfy a wide range of interests.

Artwork was specially commissioned to illustrate the entries of this first edition. Comic-book style panels were specially drawn to illustrate five myths. In addition, selected entries have black-and-white line drawings, suitable for reproduction as report covers, also specially created for this first edition of *The Lincoln Library of Greek & Roman Mythology*.

Following the text of the entry, the character's family members are identified to enable further research or to lend perspective. Multidisciplinary references were added to expand the reader's understanding of mythology and its influence on the fields of art, music, literature, science, space exploration, and word history.

Readers will find mythical allusions in William Shakespeare, Dante, English and American lit-

Reader's Guide (continued)

erature, and even modern cinema. Word histories are provided to help students recognize Mercury in the English word "merchant" and Hestia in the word "restaurant."

The Lincoln Library of Greek & Roman Mythology aims to expand the thinking of young readers. Entries are supplemented with excerpts from the key classical authors of antiquity in readable translation. Contributing editor Rick M. Newton prepared new translations of many excerpts specifically for readers of *The Lincoln Library of Greek & Roman Mythology.* For readers who want to "go to the source," citations are provided to works by Homer, Hesiod, Aeschylus, Sophocles, Euripides, Pindar, Apollonius Rhodius, Livy, Vergil, Horace, and Ovid.

In addition, group projects are supported by six plays edited for classroom presentation, depicting six different myths. To facilitate full class participation and to simulate theater of ancient Greece, the plays include roles for a chorus.

Organized and indexed as a ready-to-use reference work for those researching specific names and places, *The Lincoln Library of Greek & Roman Mythology* also supports browsing or inde-

pendent reading. Generous cross-references are provided with most entries, designed to build research skills and entice the reader to further study.

Two tables precede the Subject Index in Volume 5. The first is a table of mythological associations that links heroes, gods, and goddesses with the concepts, words, and phrases with which they are associated. The second provides a listing of English words and phrases that have their origins in Greek and Roman mythology.

Editor's Notes

A note about punctuation of possessives: The standard reference in book publishing, *The Chicago Manual of Style,* calls for the use of 's when creating possessives of proper nouns, even of those ending in s. Exceptions include names ending in -eez (such as Achilles). *The Lincoln Library of Greek & Roman Mythology* makes a further exception, bowing to general practice: when punctuating possessives for one-syllable names ending in s, such as Zeus and Mars, we have used the apostrophe alone.

Finally, myths cannot be fact-checked. Many versions of each myth have been recorded and

recounted over the centuries. The editors strove to provide coherent retellings of common versions of the myths. Comparing the renditions presented in *The Lincoln Library of Greek & Roman Mythology* to those found in other sources will spark debate and deepen understanding of the evolving nature of myth and its relationship to human imagination.

There are people and places without whose help and support *The Lincoln Library of Greek & Roman Mythology* would not have been possible. Each deserves our deepest gratitude: Rollie Welch, Young Adult Librarian, Youth Services Department, Cleveland Public Library; Arthur and Alice Gall; Patrick Bevan; Jim Corrigan and Claudia Coulton; Doug and Mary Seidner; David and Paula Stebbins; the Janes's First Light on Nantucket; The Alesci's team of Gina, Jeff, Lisa, and Dell; the A.J. Rocco's team of Brendan, Zack, Nicole, Charlie, Becca, and Addie; David Bevan, Marty Niemi, and the Indian Hill Observatory of the Chagrin Valley Astronomical Society; and especially William Seibert for giving us the opportunity to pursue this project.

CONTRIBUTORS

Editors

Timothy and Susan Gall

Contributing Editor

Rick M. Newton, Ph.D., Professor of Classics, Kent State University

Reading Consultant

Mary W. Spor, Ph.D., Professor, Alabama A&M University

Associate Editors

Sarah Kunz, Andrew Spencer

Illustrators

Linda Crockett, Joe Bromley, Randy Crider

Graphics Editor

Daniel Mehling

Assistant Editors

Krista Birnbaum, Karen Ellicott, Adam Gall, Elizabeth Gall, Jeneen Hobby, Maura Malone

Copy Editors

Jane Hoehner, Deborah A. Ring, Rosalie Wieder

Proofreaders

Jan Davis, Kristen Hampshire, Kimberly Tilly

Photo Credits

Special thanks to Alison Strum, Art Resource; British artist Maggi Hambling for allowing us to reproduce her *Minotaur Surprised While Eating*; Til Credner; Dr. Natalia Vogeikoff-Brogan, Archivist, and Caitlin Downey Verfenstein, Alison Frantz Photographic Collection, American School of Classical Studies at Athens (Greece); Jean Piety, Manager, and Rose Mary Hoge, Librarian, Science and Technology Department, Cleveland Public Library; Holly Taylor, The Toledo Museum of Art; Michael Hiles; Susan DeVictor; and Alan Bowker.

Special mention goes to Linda Crockett for the over 100 line drawings of heroes, gods, and goddesses commissioned for this set and found throughout the five volumes.

Alison Frantz Photographic Collection: 2:45, 2:58, 2:72, 3:77, 3:78, 3:79,3:79, 3:80, 3:80, 3:93, 5:87, 5:97, 5:126. Andrew Spencer: 1:35, 1:36, 1:45, 1:125, 2:6, 2:16, 2:83, 2:100, 3:46, 5:63. **Airlee Owens:** 2:87. **Constellation photographs © Til Credner/allthesky.com:** 1:17, 1:67, 1:84, 1:106, 1:114, 2:36, 2:42, 2:46, 2:50, 3:30, 3:35, 3:82, 3:106, 3:123, 4:27, 4:66, 4:107, 4:112, 5:24, 5:104. **David Graper (South Dakota State University):** 3:120. **Galen R. Frysinger:** 2:20. **Nigel P. Jones:** 3:107. **Peter Valentine, James Cook University:** 3:108. **Southeastern Regional Taxonomic Center (SERTC), South Carolina Department of Natural Resources:** 1:54, 2:59. **The Toledo Museum of Art:** 4:95, 5:62. **Art Resource, NY:** Alinari 4:68, 3:2,4:49, 2:7; Art Resource, NY 3:97, 5:45; Cameraphoto 3:58; Erich Lessing 4:91, 1:31, 1:49, 1:109, 2:4, 2:38, 2:44, 2:52, 2:81, 2:115, 2:117, 3:17, 3:19, 3:39, 3:61, 3:75, 4:5, 4:9, 4:15, 4:53, 4:80, 4:91, 5:57, 5:78, 5:79, 5:89, 5:92, 4:84, 5:13, 1:69, 5:103, 1:105, 3:47, 3:65, 4:35, 1:44, 5:19, 5:85, 5:100; Giraudon 5:83, 2:95, 5:46, 1:5; Kavaler 2:67; Nimatallah 1:39; Réunion des Musées Nationaux 2:78, 4:24, 1:7, 3:50, 3:7, 4:20, 5:42, 1:62, 1:79, 1:117, 2:22, 3:69, 3:100, 4:111, 5:33, 5:66; Scala 4:75, 1:16, 1:43, 1:71, 2:60, 2:86, 2:93, 3:13, 3:53, 3:111, 4:102, 5:69, 5:71, 5:73, 5:109, 2:75, 2:109, 1:27, 2:89, 3:89, 4:79, 5:21; Snark 5:3; Tate Gallery, London 1:97, 4:65, 5:41, 4:61; The New York Public Library 4:99; Timothy McCarthy 2:85, 4:117, 3:118, 4:46, 5:81; Vanni 1:6, 1:81, 2:101; Victoria & Albert Museum 4:31, 4:101. **R. Atkinson, University of Southern Queensland:** 1:47. **David Page:** 1:1. **Gibraltar Tourist Board:** 2:37. **Charles and Chris Krumbein:** 3:105. **Alan Bowker** (abowker@bowkera.com):

1:107. **Kimbell Art Museum:** Copyright ©2005 by Kimbell Art Museum 1:33. **Library of Congress, Prints and Photographs Division:** 1:18, 1:55, 1:57, 1:113, 2:9, 2:12, 2:18, 2:19, 2:19, 2:20, 2:27, 2:31, 2:34, 2:97, 2:107, 3:15, 3:27, 3:49, 3:50, 3:91, 4:17, 4:37, 4:71, 4:74, 4:76, 5:51, 5:112, 5:113, 5:115, 5:117. **Morgue File:** Kathy Bishop 1:53. **NASA:** 4:28; Courtesy NASA/JPL-Caltech 3:10, 5:34, 5:64, 5:69, 5:108; Dryden Flight Research Center (NASA-DFRC) 5:26; Earth Sciences and Image Analysis, Johnson Space Center 5:110; Glen Research Center (NASA-GRC) 3:87, 4:33, 4:51; Goddard Space Flight Center (NASA-GSFC) 2:43, 5:35, 5:119; International Space Station Imagery 4:47; Jet Propulsion Laboratory (NASA-JPL) 1:75, 2:35, 2:53, 3:39, 3:115, 5:39, 5:47, 5:107; Johnson Space Center (NASA-JSC) 3:34; JPL/Space Science Institute 5:75; Langley Research Center (NASA-LaRC) 2:56, 3:5; Marshall Space Flight Center (NASA-MSFC) 4:11, 4:19, 5:114; NASA, ESA, and the Hubble Heritage Team (STScI/AURA) with the acknowledgment of S. Smartt, The Queen's University of Belfast 3:73; Neil A. Armstrong 1:83. **NOAA/PMEL:** 1:93. **Royal Navy Submarine Museum:** Courtesy of The Royal Navy Submarine Museum, Gosport, England 1:1. **US Fish and Wildlife Service/ photo by James Leupold:** 5:58. **USDA image by Scott Peterson:** 1:10. *Harpers Dictionary of Classical Literature and Antiques:* 2:55, 3:1, 1:8, 1:28, 1:34, 1:37, 1:52, 1:93, 2:18, 2:39, 3:15, 3:23, 3:26, 3:102, 4:94. *Masters in Art:* 2:17, 2:15. *Museum of Antiquity Illustrated:* 5:94. *A Wonder Book, and Tanglewood Tales:* Maxfield Parrish 1:94, 2:11, 2:29, 2:69, 4:3, 4:123, 5:49. *The Mural Paintings of the Library of Congress:* Edwand Simmons 2:34, 4:43; Elihu Vedder 4:59; H.O. Walker 1:19, 2:77, 3:11, 3:34; Walter McEwan 1:4, 2:24, 3:85, 4:2.

In volume 3, page 27, the Latin lines of "O Fortuna" from *Carmina Burana* can be found in George F. Whicher, *The Goliard Poets* (New York: New Directions, 1965).

Gods and Heroes

Equivalent mythological characters

GREEK NAME	ROMAN NAME
Alexandra	Cassandra
Aphrodite	Venus
Apollo	Apollo
Ares	Mars
Artemis	Diana
Asclepius	Aesculapius
Athena	Minerva
Castor and	
Pollux	Gemini
Cronus	Saturn
Demeter	Ceres
Dionysus	Bacchus
Eos	Aurora
Eros	Cupid
Gaea	Tellus
Hades	Pluto
Helios	Sol
Hephaestus	Vulcan
Hera	Juno
Heracles	Hercules
Hermes	Mercury
Hestia	Vesta
Odysseus	Ulysses
Persephone	Proserpina
Poseidon	Neptune
Rhea	Cybele
Selene	Luna
Tyche	Fortuna
Zeus	Jupiter

See volume one, page vii, for the **Reader's Guide** to this encyclopedia. See volume five for a **Table of Associations,** linking characters to the attributes with which they are associated; a **Table of Word Origins**, listing English words and their Greek and Latin origins; and a **Subject Index**.

The Greek Alphabet

UPPERCASE	LOWERCASE	NAME	ENGLISH EQUIVALENT	SOUNDS LIKE
A	α	alpha	a	**fa**ther
B	β	beta	b	**b**ag
Γ	γ	gamma	g	**g**ain
Δ	δ	delta	d	**d**og
E	ε	epsilon	e	**e**nd
Z	ζ	zeta	z	**z**ebra
H	η	eta	ê	h**ey**
Θ	θ	theta	th	**th**ick
I	ι	iota	i	**i**t
K	κ	kappa	k	**k**ing
Λ	λ	lamda	l	**l**amp
M	μ	mu	m	**m**an
N	ν	nu	n	**n**et
Ξ	ξ	xi	ks	bo**x**
O	o	omikron	o	**o**ff
Π	π	pi	p	**p**in
P	ρ	rho	r	**r**ing
Σ	σ, ς	sigma	s	**s**ay
T	τ	tau	t	**t**op
Υ	υ	upsilon	u	p**u**t
Φ	φ	phi	f	**f**un
X	χ	chi	ch	Ba**ch**
Ψ	ψ	psi	ps	**ps**alm
Ω	ω	omega	ô	gr**ow**

The Ancient World

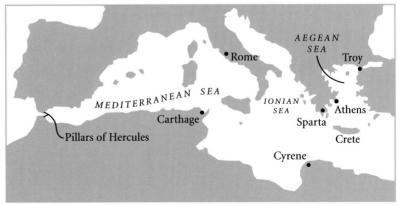

Aα

Abyla

Αβυλα

Abyla (A-buh-luh) and Calpe were two mythical mountains that, together, were known as the Pillars of Heracles. These mountains formed the two promontories (high points of land) at the western end of the Mediterranean Sea. The Greeks believed that Abyla and Calpe were formed when the great hero Heracles (Roman Hercules) tore apart a single mountain.

The two mountains stand on opposite ends of the Strait of Gibraltar, the narrow passageway that connects the Mediterranean Sea and the Atlantic Ocean. Abyla is now known as the mountain Jebel Musa in Morocco, on the northern coast of Africa.

See also Calpe; Heracles; Hercules.

Acheron

Αχερων

Acheron (A-kuh-rahn) was one of the five major rivers that flowed through the Underworld in Greek mythology. Acheron was considered to be the river of woe because its name comes from the Greek word meaning "woe" or "pain."

According to some traditions, Acheron was a son of Helios and Gaea. When the Titans had their great battle with Zeus for control of the universe, Acheron took the side of the Titans and refreshed them with drink. When Zeus and his followers defeated the Titans, Zeus punished Acheron by changing him into a river that flowed through the Underworld.

In ancient Greek geography, the name Acheron was often given to distant rivers that appeared to be at the end of the world. As those places became better known by exploration and settlement, the name was transferred to other rivers even farther away. These rivers, it was believed, provided an entrance to the lower world. Ultimately, the Acheron was placed in the lower world itself.

The Underworld, including the river Acheron, is described in Plato's *Phaedo*. Plato's descriptions are not very easy to understand.

See also Cocytus; Lethe; Phlegethon; Styx.

This submarine, launched just after the end of World War II, was named the HMS Acheron. *In the bottom picture it is shown passing under the Brooklyn Bridge in New York City. In Greek mythology, the Acheron was one of the five major rivers that flowed through the Underworld.*

Achilles

Αχιλλευς

PRONUNCIATION: uh-KIH-leez
GENDER: Male
CULTURE: Greek
ATTRIBUTES: Fearlessness; Anger; Vengeance; Speed; Short but glorious life

Valiant and lion-hearted Achilles was a Greek hero in the Trojan War. He was a mighty warrior with extraordinary strength and speed. People sometimes called him "swift-footed Achilles." Achilles' mother had held him by the heel and dipped him into the River Styx when he was a baby. The water from the river made his body invincible everywhere but the heel.

Before Achilles was born, his mother Thetis dreamed of having a son who would grow up to be a great warrior. However, an oracle told her that any child she bore would be greater than his father. Consequently, no god would marry her. Thetis had no choice but to marry a mortal man. She reluctantly agreed to marry Peleus. Soon Achilles was born. Her son, the mighty Achilles, would live a short but glorious life.

The Magic of the River Styx

Thetis wanted Achilles to be immortal and invincible, and she had an idea about how to make it so. People said that anyone who bathed in the River Styx, one of the five rivers of the Underworld, would become immortal. Achilles' mother carried him down to the banks of the River Styx, grasped him by the heel, and dipped him headfirst into the water. When she pulled him out, Achilles was howling. But from the top of his head to his ankle, Achilles was now invincible. His immortal body had just one mortal and vulnerable spot. His heel, where his mother's hand had been, had not been bathed in the water from the Styx.

Growing Strong on Meals of Entrails

Achilles' best friend was named Patroclus. The two were like brothers. From an early age, Patroclus and Achilles were trained to be warriors.

Two tutors prepared Achilles for adulthood, and Patroclus was trained along with him. One tutor was Phoenix, who was an expert in combat. Phoenix trained Achilles in the art of war. Achilles' other

In this painting by Peter Paul Rubens (1577–1640) Achilles is being dipped into the River Styx by his mother Thetis.

TRUE OR FALSE?

1. Achilles was the son of Thetis.
2. Achilles' mother tried to drown him in the River Styx.
3. Achilles and Patroclus never met.
4. Achilles was trained to be a farmer.
5. Achilles joined the Greek army when he was 15.
6. Achilles was a brave warrior in the Trojan War.
7. The only vulnerable spot on Achilles' body was his heel.
8. The Achilles tendon is located in the human arm.

tutor was Chiron, a centaur (half man, half horse). Chiron trained Achilles in the arts of music and medicine.

To make Achilles strong, Chiron stirred a pot filled with entrails—the intestines and other organs—of lions. To this mixture Chiron added the marrow of bears and wild boars. Chiron and Phoenix ladled bowls full of this special recipe for Achilles to eat for breakfast, lunch, and dinner. They believed this diet was just what Achilles needed to grow strong and brave for battle.

Both Achilles and Patroclus were brave but Achilles was the stronger of the two. Patroclus never stopped trying to prove that he was as brave in battle as Achilles. This drive to compete with Achilles would one day lead Patroclus to take a dangerous risk and meet a tragic end.

Can Thetis Stop the Prophecy from Coming True?

When Achilles was only nine years old, the seer Calchas made a prediction: Calchas prophesied that the Greeks would never defeat the city of Troy, the capital of a neighboring empire, without the help of Achilles.

Achilles was a young man when there was talk of a war with Troy. Achilles' mother Thetis remembered the prophecy and knew that the Greeks would want Achilles to fight with them. She wanted to protect her son from the dangers and horrors of war and she knew the Greek army would soon be looking for him. Thetis decided to hide Achilles so she disguised him as a girl and sent him to live among the young maidens in the court of King Lycomedes of Scyros.

Thetis's plan to keep Achilles hidden did not work for long. Odysseus, king of Ithaca, was the most clever and cunning of all the Greeks. He knew the Greeks needed Achilles to help them win the war with Troy.

Odysseus heard rumors that Achilles was hiding in Scyros. Disguised as a peddler, the wily Odysseus went to Scyros with a plan to find Achilles. First he found the marketplace near Lycomedes' palace. Then he spread out his wares—including a shield and spear—for all the members of

Lycomedes' court to see. The young maidens approached, eager to see what the peddler was offering. When they saw the weapons, all the maidens drew away in fear—except one.

Although Achilles was dressed as a girl, he was still a trained warrior. His strong fist shot forward and grabbed the weapons. A smile broke over Odysseus's face—his plan had worked. Only a warrior would be so interested in weapons. Achilles' actions revealed the warrior beneath his flowing girl's dress. Achilles, just 15 years old, was strong and hungry for battle. He could not resist the lure of Odysseus's shiny spear. Odysseus stood before Achilles and asked him to join the Greeks in battle against Troy. Achilles tossed away his girl's clothes and agreed to follow Odysseus to war.

On to Troy

With Achilles on their side, the Greeks began planning their attack on Troy. Even Phoenix, Achilles' early teacher, remained loyal and

This oil painting by the Flemish artist Peter Paul Rubens (1577–1640) shows the battle between the Greek Achilles and the Trojan Hector. They fought during the Trojan War, and Achilles won the battle.

followed Achilles to war against the Trojans.

The Greek army assembled more than 1,000 ships and prepared to sail. Agamemnon, the king of Mycenae, was the commander. Soon his army was ready for battle.

When they arrived at Troy, the Greeks discovered that the Trojans were hard to defeat. Battle after battle ended in a standstill. For years the war raged, but victory proved elusive.

Although they could not capture the great city itself, they laid waste to the surrounding country-

side. Achilles and his mighty warriors sacked city after city. After nine years of fighting, the Greeks had destroyed twelve cities around Troy.

As a reward for his victories, Achilles received a beautiful slave girl named Briseis. He cherished her as a symbol of his victories, just like an athlete cherishes a trophy received for winning a race.

A God Turns Against the Greeks

Agamemnon, the leader of the Greek army, also wanted a trophy of war, so he took the slave girl

Achilles (continued)

Chryseis. She was the daughter of one of the priests who served Apollo, the god of light and music. When his daughter was taken, the priest was heartbroken. The priest begged Agamemnon to return his daughter, but the arrogant Agamemnon refused.

The priest then turned to Apollo for help. Apollo saw that the priest was suffering over the loss of his daughter and knew that Agamemnon deserved to be punished. Apollo sent a terrible plague on the Greeks. Apollo's golden arrows poured down on the Greek army and burned them. Agamemnon soon learned he had made a powerful enemy.

A Battle of Wills

The Trojan War dragged on. It was now ten years since the Greek army had left home. Agamemnon struggled to maintain morale among his soldiers. Many were homesick and tired and wanted to go back to Greece. Having Apollo angry with Agamemnon just made things worse. Agamemnon felt desperate. He had to do something to

This painting adorns a palace known as the Achilleion, built by Austrian Empress Elizabeth on the Greek island of Corfu. Achilles is shown dragging the body of Hector around the walls of Troy. The painting is by Austrian artist Frans Matsch.

In this dramatic painting by the French painter Joseph-Benoit Suvee (1743–1807), Achilles drops the body of Hector on the ground at the foot of the body of Patroclus.

improve conditions and morale for his troops. So he reluctantly freed his slave girl, Chryseis.

But Agamemnon was a proud leader. With Chryseis gone, he felt a symbol of his leadership was lost. Agamemnon wanted another prize of war, so he took Briseis away from Achilles. Achilles was outraged. The injustice was too much to bear and Achilles sought a way to punish Agamemnon.

Agamemnon may have been the leader of the Greek army, but Achilles was its greatest warrior. Achilles could no longer control the anger he felt, so he confronted Agamemnon. He drew his spear and was just about to thrust it into Agamemnon when Athena, the goddess of war and wisdom, appeared. Athena grabbed Achilles by the hair and pulled him away.

The goddess promised Achilles even greater prizes and trophies if he would suppress his rage and spare Agamemnon. Achilles agreed to let Agamemnon live, but his urge to punish Agamemnon was not yet satisfied.

Still angry, Achilles left the battlefield and went back to his tent. He refused to join the Greeks in the battle against the Trojans. Even when the Greek ships were being burned and the Greek army was being routed, Achilles stayed in his tent. Without Achilles, the Greeks began to lose.

Will Achilles Ever Fight Again?

Achilles sat brooding alone in his tent, his armor piled up on the floor, while the Trojan army crushed the Greeks. Meanwhile, Patroclus,

Achilles (continued)

Achilles' boyhood friend, was devising a plan.

Achilles was the warrior who terrified his enemies, and Patroclus had a lifelong dream to do the same. Patroclus believed that the Trojan warriors would tremble with fear if he approached them, clad in Achilles' armor. Patroclus went to Achilles and begged for the chance to wear Achilles' armor into battle. After some convincing, Achilles agreed.

Patroclus put on the armor of Achilles, strode out of the tent, and jumped into Achilles' chariot. The Trojans panicked when they saw Achilles' chariot advancing. They thought Achilles himself was driving the chariot and they fled. Patroclus and his band of Greek warriors drove the Trojans off the burning Greek ships. Trojan warriors scattered in all directions, with the Greek warriors in pursuit.

Suddenly Patroclus found himself alone, facing Hector, the son of Troy's king Priam. Hector thought he was facing the mighty Achilles, so he attacked with fury. The two warriors drew their weapons and flew into battle. Hector was strong in combat, but so was Patroclus. Patroclus let his guard down for only a moment and Hector saw his chance. Hector drove his lance through Patroclus, piercing his heart. Patroclus groaned in agony and fell to the battlefield. Achilles' beloved friend was dead.

When Patroclus did not return from battle, Achilles questioned the other warriors. The news that his friend was dead shook Achilles with grief and anger. He swore to take revenge on Hector, but he had no armor—Patroclus was wearing his armor when he died. From miles away Achilles' mother sensed her son's grief and came to his aid. Thetis convinced Hephaestus, the god of fire and blacksmithing, to make Achilles a new suit of armor.

The Warrior Returns

Wearing his new armor and with revenge on his mind, Achilles marched off to look for Hector, Patroclus's killer. At the sight of Achilles in his dazzling new armor, the Trojan warriors scattered in all directions.

Priam had forbidden his youngest and favorite son Polydorus from fighting in the Trojan War. Polydorus was one of Troy's fastest runners and he liked to show off his speed. The day Achilles returned to the battlefield, Polydorus was running in and out among the Trojan warriors on the battlefield, not engaging in battle but running for the joy of it. The fleet-footed Achilles was looking for Hector, but when he saw Polydorus, he saw his chance to punish Priam's family. Polydorus was a swift runner, but so was Achilles. He pursued Polydorus until he caught up with him. Achilles then thrust his spear right through Polydorus's body. Priam had lost his favorite son to Achilles.

By now most of the Trojan warriors had fled to safety behind the walls of Troy. Hector alone stayed to face the wrath of Achilles. Achilles pursued Hector around and around the walls of Troy.

Priam before Achilles.

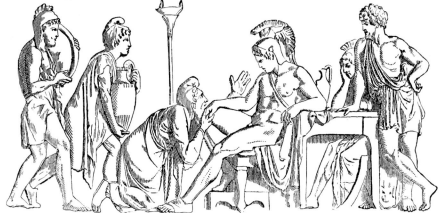

Finally Achilles cornered Hector and the fierce battle began. The two warriors fought bravely. At last Achilles prevailed, slaying Hector. But Achilles wasn't satisfied. His rage over the death of Patroclus still burned and he wanted to punish Hector further. Achilles tied Hector's dead body to the back of his chariot and dragged it around the walls of Troy.

Achilles had avenged the death of Patroclus. Now it was the Trojans' turn to mourn. Priam, the king of Troy, had lost two sons, and it hurt him deeply to to see Hector's body treated with so little respect. Hector had died honorably in battle and Priam felt he deserved an honorable burial.

The proud king went to Achilles' tent to beg for Hector's body. The king offered boundless ransom in exchange for his son's body.

Moved by the sight of the aged father begging for the corpse of his son, Achilles felt great pity. For that moment the great warrior forgot his rage and bitter grief over the death of Patroclus. He thought of his own father, whom he would never see again. Although the two were enemies, Priam and Achilles hugged each other and sobbed heavily over the losses war had caused them. Achilles gave Hector's body back to Priam, but Hector's death had not stopped the war. Fierce fighting was still taking place.

The Cycle of Revenge Continues

One of Hector's younger brothers was Paris, the handsome Trojan who had abducted Helen and started the Trojan War. Paris avoided engaging in battle whenever he could, but his aim with a bow and arrow was deadly accurate. After Hector's burial and Polydorus's death, Paris picked up his bow, slung a quiver of arrows over his shoulder, and set off to settle his family's score with Achilles.

Paris pursued Achilles until he was close enough to draw his bow. When he had a clear view of Achilles, Paris pulled back the

Achilles (continued)

bow. His arrow flew high into the air and came down to hit Achilles as he was running away. Paris thought his shot had failed since it hit Achilles on the heel. He did not know that his aim could not have been better because the heel was the only vulnerable spot on Achilles' body. The heel was the spot where his mother's hand had held the baby Achilles when she dipped him into the River Styx.

Paris was stunned to see Achilles fall to the ground, dead, from the wound to his heel. Greece had lost its greatest warrior.

For seventeen days the Greeks mourned Achilles and Patroclus, their two fallen heroes. The Greeks then placed the bodies of their heroes on a funeral pyre, burned them, and buried their ashes together.

FAMILY: Father was Peleus, king of the Myrmidons; mother was Thetis, a Nereid (sea nymph).

IN ART: Achilles was often depicted on vases created by Greek potters during the sixth and seventh centuries B.C.—about 2,700 years ago. One of the most famous of these vase paintings depicts Achilles and his fellow Greek warrior Ajax relaxing after a day of battle. The two are playing dice, an ancient game similar to backgammon. Famous artists such as Flemish seven-teenth-century painter Peter Paul Rubens and French nineteenth-century painter Eugène Delacroix have also painted Achilles. Achilles is almost always shown wearing armor and holding a spear.

IN LITERATURE: Achilles is the central figure and epic hero of Homer's *Iliad*. From the very beginning of this epic poem, it is clear that Achilles is an angry and vengeful character. As with many ancient poets, Homer begins his poem by asking for divine inspiration. The *Iliad* opens with these lines:

> Sing, goddess, the wrath of Peleus' son Achilles, that deadly wrath which brought countless woes to the Greeks.
>
> *Iliad, translation by Rick M. Newton*

When Achilles learned that his best friend, Patroclus, had been killed, Achilles was grief-stricken. Achilles did not hesitate to show his intense emotions. In the *Iliad* Homer describes the scene where Achilles first learns of Patroclus's death:

> A black cloud of grief enshrouded him. With his two hands he grabbed the dirt from the ground and poured it over his head, soiling the beauty of his face. He lay in the dust, sprawling with his entire body, and tore his hair with both hands.
>
> *Iliad, book 18, lines 23–27; translation by Rick M. Newton*

The scientific name for yarrow, Achillea, comes from Achilles.

The Elizabethan poet William Shakespeare mentions Achilles in several of his plays including *Love's Labour's Lost, The Rape of Lucrece, Troilus and Cressida,* and *Henry IV Part 2*. In *Henry IV Part 2*, Achilles' spear is described as being able to both kill and cure, because King Telephus was wounded by the spear and learned that he could only be cured by the same thing that wounded him.

> That gold must round engirt these brows of mine,
> Whose smile and frown, like to Achilles' spear,
> Is able with the change to kill and cure.

The story of Achilles has also inspired modern poets including the twentieth-century English poet

*"Sing, goddess, the wrath of Peleus' son Achilles,
that deadly wrath which brought countless woes
to the Greeks."*

—Homer's *Iliad*

W. H. Auden. The final stanza of his poem, *The Shield of Achilles,* reads:

> The thin-lipped armorer,
>   Hephaestus, hobbled away,
> Thetis of the shining breasts
>   Cried out in dismay
> At what the god had wrought
>   To please her son, the strong
> Iron-hearted man-slaying Achilles
>   Who would not live long.

Jonathan Shay's *Achilles in Vietnam* (1994) draws comparisons between the experiences of Achilles in the Trojan War and those of soldiers who fought in the Vietnam War (1965–73). The Trojan War occurred almost 3,200 years before the Vietnam War, but Shay believed that Homer's descriptions in the *Iliad* are common to all wars, which destroy men's character through prolonged violence and traumatic shock.

IN SPACE: In 1906, the German astronomer Max Wolf discovered a group of asteroids within the orbit of Jupiter. He named them the Trojan group, and named one of the asteroids Achilles.

IN SCIENCE: The scientific name for the flower yarrow is A*chillea millefolium.* Achilles is said to have used yarrow on his soldiers' wounds during the Trojan War. Yarrow is considered an herbal remedy today.

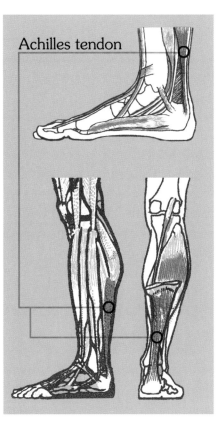

Achilles tendon

The Achilles tendon in the human leg.

WORD HISTORY: In modern speech, the term *Achilles' heel* is used to refer to the biggest weakness of a person who is otherwise strong and invincible.

MODERN USAGE: On the human body, the tendon that connects the calf muscle to the heel bone is called the Achilles tendon, after the story of Achilles, who was the fastest runner of the Greeks. "Achilles tendonitis" is a common

injury among runners and other athletes. Many running clubs are named after Achilles. An annual fundraising marathon for disabled athletes held in New York City is called the Achilles Marathon.

GO TO THE SOURCE: Homer's epic poem the *Iliad* focuses on Achilles as the greatest heroic Greek soldier. Achilles also appears in the play *Iphigenia at Aulis* by Euripides.

Acis

Ακις

Acis (AH-kihs) was a handsome shepherd in Greek mythology. He lived on the island of Sicily, just south of Italy. Acis was loved by Galatea, a sea nymph. However, Polyphemus, a fearsome cyclops (one-eyed giant), was also in love with Galatea.

One day Polyphemus found Acis and Galatea together. In a jealous rage, the cyclops tore a rock from Mount Etna and threw it at Acis. The boulder crushed the shepherd's skull, killing him instantly. Galatea transformed the flow of blood that seeped from beneath the boulder into a river.

See also Etna, Mount; Polyphemus.

Acrisius

Ακρισιος

PRONUNCIATION: uh-KRIH-see-uhs
GENDER: Male
CULTURE: Greek
ATTRIBUTES: Worrying; Trying to avoid fate

Acrisius, king of Argos, could not escape the oracle's prediction: he was accidentally killed by his own grandson, Perseus.

In Greek mythology, Acrisius was the king of Argos. Like most kings, Acrisius wanted a son to be the heir to the throne. Acrisius grew older and older, but his only child was a daughter, the beautiful Danae.

Danae was a joy to the people of Argos, but Acrisius could not love her because of his desire for a son. In desperation Acrisius traveled to Delphi to ask the oracle (priestess of Apollo) how he could find a male heir. The priestess told Acrisius his destiny: One day Danae would give birth to a son who would kill his grandfather.

Could Acrisius Lock Away the Prophecy?

Acrisius was terrified by this prediction. He vowed that Danae would never become pregnant. To protect against the fulfillment of the prophecy, Acrisius ordered an underground bronze chamber to be built. He locked Danae inside. But Acrisius underestimated the power of the gods.

Zeus, the king of the Olympian gods, saw Danae through a tiny crack in the roof of her bronze chamber and fell in love with her. Transforming himself into a shower of golden rain, Zeus visited Danae. Soon after Zeus' visit, Danae realized she was pregnant.

When Acrisius learned that Danae was pregnant with the son of Zeus, he had the bronze chamber pulled out of the ground.

Danae gave birth to a son. She named him Perseus. Acrisius trembled with fear at the sight of his grandson. Every time he looked at the infant, he thought of the oracle's words. Unable to overcome his fear, Acrisius trapped both mother and child inside a wooden chest. He nailed the chest closed and threw it out to sea. Danae and Perseus would surely die. He was now safe from the prophecy. At last, Acrisius could relax.

Zeus, seeing the chest floating on the stormy sea asked Poseidon to calm the water. Poseidon, the god of the sea, granted Zeus' request. The surface of the sea became as smooth as glass. The chest bobbed gently in the water until it washed ashore on the island of Seriphos. A fisherman named Dictys found Danae and Perseus on the beach. He took them home and cared for them.

Perseus grew up to be a strong and brave young man. He acom-

TRUE OR FALSE?

1. Acrisius was the duke of Argos.
2. Acrisius had seven daughters and seven sons.
3. Danae was hated by the people of Argos.
4. Acrisius locked Danae and Perseus in a wooden chest.
5. Perseus intentionally killed his grandfather, Acrisius.
6. Poseidon made the seas rage to keep Danae and Perseus from reaching the island of Seriphos.

Discus Throwing and Mathematics

In Greek mythology Perseus accidently killed his grandfather when his discus flew into a crowd of spectators. Discus throwing was a popular ancient sport. In the modern world, the discus throw is still a popular track and field event. How far the discus goes is more a matter of speed than strength, as the following calculations illustrate.

The thrower must release the discus when the arm is at a right angle to the direction in which the discus must travel.

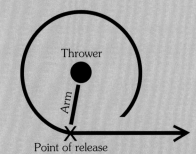

A good discus thrower with a strong arm can also use that arm as a whip to apply more speed to the discus. Increasing the speed of rotation is the most important thing the thrower can do to improve his or her discus throws.

Source: Bill Willis, Worsley School, Alberta, Canada

Throwing a discus is unlike most other throws, in that the majority of the speed imparted to the discus comes from the rotation of the thrower's body, not from "throwing." In order to throw a discus well, the thrower must rotate very fast, and let go of the discus at just the right instant. The following calculations illustrate how much speed is involved.

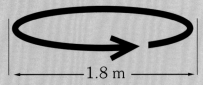

1.8 m

For simplicity, assume the thrower can rotate his or her body, with the arm extended holding the discus, in a circle that is 1.8 metres wide.

The total distance covered by the discus during the final rotation will be the circumference (C) of this circle above, or 5.65 metres.

$$C = \pi \times d$$
$$= \pi \times 1.8$$
$$= 5.65m$$

If the thrower can make that last rotation in a time of just one second, the discus will travel 5.65 m in one second. Its speed v will be 5.65 m/s, as calculated below.

$$V = \frac{distance}{time}$$
$$= \frac{5.65m}{1sec}$$
$$= 5.65m/s = 20.3km/h$$

This is the speed at which the discus will leave the thrower's hand.

plished many heroic tasks and his fame spread throughout all of Greece.

A Discus Delivers the Prophecy's Death Blow

Many years later, Acrisius heard tales about a great discus thrower named Perseus. Could this be Perseus, Danae's son? Acrisius's curiosity led him to join a large crowd gathered to watch the discus competition. From his place in the crowd he gazed upon the figure of Perseus.

Handsome, confident, clever, and athletic, Perseus stood among the competitors. When his turn came he picked up the discus and took his place on the field.

Perseus coiled back, spun with his arm extended, and launched the discus with lightning speed. But the discus went wide and flew into the crowd where Acrisius was standing. In horror Acrisius saw it coming, but it was too late. The discus struck him and he fell to the ground, dead.

Perseus had unknowingly fulfilled the prophecy. He had accidentally killed his own grandfather. The oracle is known to speak the truth and Acrisius could not escape his fate.

See also Danae; Perseus.

FAMILY: Father was Abas.

Actaeon

Ακταιων

PRONUNCIATION: AK-tee-ahn
GENDER: Male
CULTURE: Greek
ATTRIBUTES: Hunting

Actaeon was a skilled hunter. One day he spied Artemis, the Greek goddess of the hunt, bathing in a pond of water in the forest. This angered Artemis. To punish Actaeon, Artemis turned him into a deer. His fifty dogs, unable to recognize their master, tore Actaeon to pieces.

Actaeon's mother sent him at an early age to study hunting with Chiron, the wisest of all centaurs. (A centaur is half man, half horse.) Chiron was also the teacher of the Greek hero Achilles. With Chiron's training, Actaeon became a cunning hunter.

Actaeon Accidentally Spies on Artemis

Actaeon grew to be a fine hunter. He hunted with fifty hunting dogs. One day, after a long hunt, Actaeon and his dogs went in search of water. Actaeon needed to quench his thirst. He came upon a pool of water, but a group of young maidens was bathing there. Actaeon wasn't trying to spy on them, but he could not help what he saw.

One of the maidens bathing was Artemis, the goddess of the hunt. Her companions attempted to shield the goddess with their bodies, but she was much taller than any of them and could not be hidden.

Actaeon Changes from Master to Prey

When Artemis saw Actaeon looking at her exposed body, she flew into a rage. Artemis scooped up a handful of water and flung it at Actaeon. A pair of antlers sprouted from the spots on his forehead where the water touched. Within a few moments, Actaeon was com-pletely transformed into a deer. His dogs no longer recognized their master, but instead saw him as prey. Terrified, Actaeon fled. His fifty well-trained dogs pursued him. He tried and tried, but Actaeon had no power to call them off. The dogs caught Actaeon and tore his body to pieces.

The "Dog Days of Summer"

In ancient times, hunters remembered the story of Actaeon. They were careful not to anger Artemis and were wary of wandering too near to the pools of water found in the forest. Instead, hunters erected statues of Actaeon and dedicated them to protecting hunters from extreme summer heat. One explanation for calling the hottest days of summer the *dog days of sum-*

TRUE OR FALSE?

1. Actaeon was known as a great shepherd.
2. Artemis changed Actaeon into a deer.
3. Actaeon was killed by a hunter's arrow.
4. Hunters built statues of Actaeon as protection from summer heat.
5. Actaeon had a dog named Laelaps.
6. There is a mountain named in honor of Actaeon.

mer is because Actaeon was with his fifty hunting dogs when he was searching for water on a hot summer day. Another explanation comes from the time of year, the hottest days, when the constellation Canis Major ("The Great Dog") rises in the sky.

FAMILY: Father was Aristaeus; mother was Autonoe; grandfather was Apollo.

IN ART: The story of Actaeon has inspired many artists. Actaeon is often depicted at the moment when he first sees the Greek goddess Artemis, or during the attack by his hunting dogs. The Italian Renaissance painter Titian made the story of Actaeon the subject of several paintings in the 1550s and 1560s.

IN LITERATURE: The poem *Actaeon* by nineteenth-century English poet Alfred Noyes tells the story of Actaeon's tragic death. Two other English poets writing a century earlier referred to Actaeon. Poet Cornelius Webb mentions the death of Actaeon in his poem *Queen-Beauty of the Night.* The poem *Adonais* by Percy Bysshe Shelley uses Actaeon's death as a reference in this stanza:

> he, as I guess,
> Had gaz'd on Nature's naked loveliness,
> Actaeon-like, and now he fled astray
> With feeble steps o'er the world's wilderness,
> And his own thoughts, along that rugged way,
> Pursu'd, like raging hounds, their father and their prey.

Even earlier, in the Elizabethan age, Shakespeare proves he is familiar with the myth of Actaeon by comparing his character Master Ford in *The Merry Wives of Windsor,* to "Sir Actaeon with Ringwood at his heels." In *Twelfth Night* Shakespeare refers to the attack of Actaeon's hounds, when the character Duke Orsino says:

> O, when mine eyes did see Olivia first,
> Methought she purged the air of pestilence.
> That instant was I turn'd into a hart;
> And my desires, like fell and cruel hounds,
> E'er since pursue me.

Actaeon (continued)

An ancient wall carving showing Actaeon being torn apart by his hunting dogs.

IN SPACE: The constellation Canis Major is associated with Laelaps, one of Actaeon's dogs.

MODERN USAGE: Saint Helena, an island British territory in the Atlantic Ocean off the west coast of Africa, is home to two mountains—Mount Actaeon and Diana Peak. (Diana is the Roman name for Artemis.)

English pianist and composer Sir Richard Rodney Bennet composed *Actaeon* for horn and orchestra in 1977.

GO TO THE SOURCE: The story of Actaeon can by found in book 3 of Ovid's *Metamorphoses* and in book 3 of the *Library* by Apollodorus.

Admetus

Αδμητος

Admetus (ad-MEE-tuhs) was the king of Thessaly in Greek mythology. Like most kings, he had a large flock of sheep that needed tending. Most kings have a lowly servant to tend their sheep. Admetus had the great god Apollo tend his.

How did Admetus get Apollo to tend his sheep? Apollo—the god of light, music, poetry, and reason—killed the cyclopes. This angered Zeus. As punishment, Zeus made Apollo tend Admetus's sheep for one year. Apollo became Admetus's servant.

Admetus and Alcestis

Admetus wanted to marry Alcestis. However, her father, Pelias, said Admetus could only take his daughter away if he drove a chariot drawn by lions and bears. Apollo agreed to help. Apollo used his powers to produce a team of wild beasts to pull Admetus's chariot. When Admetus arrived, driving his chariot, Pelias helped his daughter climb in. Admetus and Alcestis were married.

Admetus is Saved from Death

As time went on Admetus became deathly ill. Apollo asked the gods to save Admetus, his mortal master, from death. The gods agreed, but on one condition: that Admetus find someone who would be willing to die in his place. Admetus accepted the gods' offer, thinking surely one of his soldiers would give his life for his king. At first Admetus was not worried, but when no one stepped forward, willing to die in his place, Admetus became concerned.

A Devoted Wife Makes the Ultimate Sacrifice and Is Rewarded by a Hero

As time went on Admetus's illness worsened. Still no one offered to die for him; not even his parents, who were old and had only a short time to live. Finally his devoted wife, Alcestis, agreed to die in her husband's place.

As Admetus grew well, Alcestis grew ill. Just at this time, the Greek hero Heracles arrived at the palace. He was saddened at the sight of Alcestis dying. He decided to rescue her from eternal death in the Underworld. When Death came to take Alcestis, Heracles seized him, and forced him to give up Alcestis. Thus, Admetus and Alcestis were reunited.

See also Alcestis.

Canis Major: The Great Dog

The constellation Canis Major shows one of the hunting dogs of either Actaeon or Orion. The brightest star in Canis Major is (1) Sirius. The name Sirius comes from the Greek word for "scorching."

Because of its position within Canis Major, Sirius has also been called the "dog star." Sirius composes the dog's head. This star is about 23 times brighter than the Sun, and only 8.6 light-years from Earth.

In ancient Egypt, Sirius rose above the horizon every year at the same time that the waters of the Nile River rose. The Egyptians also recognized that Sirius rose during the hottest days of summer. This is one origin of the phrase "dog days of summer."

The Egyptians thought this star symbolized the god Anubis, the god of mummification who had the head of a jackal.

Till Credner/allthesky.com

Adonis

Αδωνις

PRONUNCIATION: uh-DAHN-ihs
GENDER: Male
CULTURE: Greek
ATTRIBUTES: Beauty; Shortness of
life

Adonis was one of the most beautiful mortal men who ever lived. He was especially dear to Aphrodite, the goddess of love and passion. When Adonis was killed by a wild boar, Aphrodite was grief-stricken. She turned every drop of his blood into a bright red flower now known as the *anemone*.

Adonis was the son of Smyrna, a princess. Before Adonis was born, the goddess Aphrodite made Smyrna fall in love with her own father, Cinyras, the king of Cyprus. Aphrodite cast a spell over Cinyras so that he could not recognize his own daughter. The two were married, and Smyrna soon became pregnant. Twelve days later, Cinyras, to his horror, realized that Smyrna was his own daughter!

Smyrna Escapes Murder

Cinyras was angry because of Aphrodite's spell. He took his wrath

out on his daughter. Cinyras drew his sword and chased Smyrna all over the royal palace. Cinyras cornered Smyrna and raised his sword to strike her. Cowering, Smyrna prayed to the gods for help. The gods took pity on her and turned her into a tree.

Even though she was now a tree, Smyrna was still pregnant.

This painting depicts Aphrodite and Cupid mourning over a dead Adonis.

The baby continued to grow beneath her bark. The ancient Greeks called the tree *smyrna* after the poor princess. Smyrna was used by the ancients as a burial spice for the dead.

Who Will Win Adonis?

After many months passed the trunk of the smyrna tree split open. The cries of a baby could be heard all over Cyprus. The women of the island rushed to find the infant in distress. Aphrodite, the goddess of love, also heard the cries and went to Cyprus to investigate. When Aphrodite arrived, she found the women pulling a beautiful baby

TRUE OR FALSE?

1. Adonis was known as the most beautiful mortal.
2. Adonis was the son of Smyrna.
3. Aphrodite and Persephone fought over Adonis.
4. Adonis married Persephone.
5. Adonis was killed by a wolf.
6. William Shakespeare wrote a poem about Adonis.
7. There is a star named for Adonis.

boy from the trunk of the tree. Aphrodite was stunned by the baby's beauty and decided to keep him for her own. Aphrodite named the baby Adonis.

Aphrodite hid the baby in a chest. She wanted to keep his beauty for herself. She took the chest to Persephone, goddess of the Underworld, for safekeeping. Aphrodite gave a stern warning to Persephone not to open the chest.

Persephone wanted to respect Aphrodite's wishes, but the temptation was too great. She wanted to know what was inside the chest! She carefully lifted the lid. When Persephone's eye caught sight of baby Adonis, she, too, was dazzled by his beauty. Persephone vowed to keep Adonis for her own.

When Aphrodite returned to the Underworld, Persephone refused to return Adonis. Enraged, Aphrodite refused to leave the Underworld without Adonis. The two goddesses fought bitterly over who would keep the baby.

Finally Zeus, king of the gods, settled the dispute: each year of Adonis's life would be divided three ways. He would spend four months with Aphrodite, four months with Persephone, and four months on his own.

Adonis and Aphrodite Together, but Not for Long

As he grew older, Adonis grew even more beautiful. At first he enjoyed equally the time he spent with Aphrodite and Persephone. But as time went on, he fell in love with Aphrodite. He gave up his time with Persephone and devoted eight months of each year to Aphrodite. Finally Adonis gave up his four months alone and spent all of his time with Aphrodite. They were a devoted couple, spending their days contentedly lounging in the shade of a tree.

This mural in the Library of Congress in Washington, D.C. shows Adonis after he has been killed by a wild boar. The poet Shakespeare's name is above the mural because he wrote a famous poem about Adonis.

Sometimes Aphrodite joined Adonis, a skilled hunter, on expeditions. One day when Adonis went hunting, he tracked a giant boar and shot it with his arrows. The boar fell to the ground. Adonis approached to retrieve the carcass, but the boar was still alive. Adonis was taken completely by surprise. The boar snorted and struggled to its feet. Head down, it plunged forward and gored Adonis with its tusks. Adonis fell, bleeding, and died of the wounds.

Aphrodite was heartbroken. In grief, she turned each drop of Adonis's blood into a bright red flower. Aphrodite begged the gods to allow her to keep his body with her during the spring and summer, and to allow her to spend the fall and winter with him in the Underworld.

The Greeks used the story of Adonis to explain the passing of the seasons. Adonis, a beautiful mortal whose life was short, represents the spring season.

FAMILY: Son of Cinyras, the king of Cyprus, and his daughter, Smyrna.

IN ART: In painting and sculpture, Adonis is depicted as a handsome, muscular young man. He is often shown alongside Aphrodite.

IN LITERATURE: The famous lovers are celebrated in William Shakespeare's romantic poem *Venus and Adonis.* (Venus is the Roman name for Aphrodite.) The first stanza reads:

> Even as the sun with purple-
>   colour'd face
> Had ta'en his last leave of the
>   weeping morn,
> Rose-cheek'd Adonis hied him to
>   the chase;
> Hunting he loved, but love he
>   laugh'd to scorn;
> Sick-thoughted Venus makes amain
>   unto him,

And like a bold-faced suitor 'gins to woo him.

The death of Adonis is mentioned in book 1 of the epic poem *Paradise Lost* by seventeenth-century English poet John Milton:

> While smooth Adonis from his
>   native rock
> Ran purple to the sea, suppos'd
>   with blood.

The poet Percy Bysshe Shelley alludes to the story of Adonis in the poem *Adonais: An Elegy on the Death of John Keats.* Shelley mourns the death of his friend:

> I weep for Adonais—he is dead!
> Oh, weep for Adonais! though our
>   tears
> Thaw not the frost which binds so
>   dear a head!

IN SPACE: Adonis is the name of an asteroid that crosses the orbits of Mars and Earth. Adonis passed within 1.2 million miles (2 million kilometers) of Earth in 1936, which made it a near-miss by astronomical standards. The Adonis asteroid was not spotted again until 1977. ADONIS is also an acronym for the Adaptive Optics Near Infra-red System, and also for the Adaptive Optics New Intelligent System,

Adonis, Aphrodite's lover, was slain by a wild boar.

two telescopes used for infra-red images of space.

WORD HISTORY: The term *Adonis* is used when referring to an extremely handsome man.

MODERN USAGE: According to legend, the red rose was created when the blood of Adonis stained a white rose.

GO TO THE SOURCE: The love story of Venus and Adonis is retold in book 10 of Ovid's *Metamorphoses,* and is mentioned in book 3 of the *Library* by Apollodorus. (Venus is the Roman name for the goddess, Aphrodite.)

Adrasteia

Αδραστεια

In Greek mythology, Adrasteia (ah-DRAH-stee-uh) was one of the gentle nymphs who lived on the island of Crete and cared for Zeus when he was a baby.

See also Nymphs; Rhea; Zeus.

Aeacus

Αιακος

PRONUNCIATION: EE-ah-kuhs
GENDER: Male
CULTURE: Greek
ATTRIBUTES: Justice; Judge of the Underworld

Aeacus lived alone on an island. To keep him from being lonely, Zeus, the Greek king of the gods, transformed the ants on the island into warrior men. These warriors were known as the Myrmidons, and Aeacus became their king. When he died, Aeacus was selected as a judge of the Underworld.

Aeacus was king of the Myrmidons in life and a judge of the Underworld in death. His father was Zeus, the most powerful of the Greek gods, and his mother was Aegina, a nymph. The story of Aeacus's birth is this: One day Zeus looked down to Earth from Mount Olympus and spied Aegina, a beautiful woman, and fell deeply in love. To keep their love a secret, Zeus carried Aegina off to a nearby island. Soon after, Aegina gave birth to a son. She named the baby Aeacus.

Aeacus Needs Some Friends

For the first few years of his life, Aeacus had only his mother for company, for they were the only people living on the island. Aegina eventually died of old age, leaving Aeacus alone. Zeus pitied his lonely son and decided to give the young man some companions. Zeus transformed the ants on the island into people. These people came to be known as the Myrmidons. The name Myrmidon comes from *myrmikes,* the Greek word for ants.

Wise Aeacus Decides the Fates of Others

The Myrmidons made Aeacus, a kind and honorable man, their king. King Aeacus named his island home Aegina in honor of his mother. The Myrmidons became mighty and obedient warriors. Aeacus, their king, was known as one of the most just kings in all of Greece. Even Zeus recognized his son's wisdom and fairness. Zeus called on Aeacus to decide arguments between the gods themselves. After Aeacus died, the gods made Aeacus—with Minos and Rhadamanthus—one of the three judges of the Underworld.

See also Myrmidons.

FAMILY: Father was Zeus; mother was Aegina, the daughter of a river-god.

GO TO THE SOURCE: The story of Aeacus can be found in book 3 chapter 12 of the *Library* by Apollodorus. Aeacus is also mentioned in Hesiod's *Theogony* and

TRUE OR FALSE?

1. Aeacus was the son of Zeus.
2. Zeus turned goats into men so Aeacus would not be lonely.
3. Aeacus became the king of the Myrmidons.
4. Aeacus was a cruel and unfair king.
5. The gods appointed Aeacus as a judge in the Underworld.

Myrmidons: The Ants Became an Army

The ants on the island of Aegina were turned into mighty warriors by Zeus. They were called the Myrmidons and became famous throughout Greece. The name Myrmidon comes from *myrmikes*, the Greek word for ants.

Myrm's Ant Nest - www.antnest.co.uk

This close-up shows two ants locked in battle. In fact, many types of ants are warriors, just like the Myrmidons. Ants can sense when an enemy has entered the nest and will fight to the death to protect their home.

Scientists also use the Greek word *myrmi* to name ants. The ant in the picture to the right is a type of ant that scientists call *Myrmoteras undet.*

Scientists have classified all living things on Earth into categories. The ant *Myrmoteras undet* is classified as follows:

KINGDOM: *Animalia*
PHYLUM: *Arthropoda*
SUBPHYLUM: *Hexapoda*
CLASS: *Insecta*
SUBCLASS: *Pterygota*
INFRACLASS: *Neoptera*
ORDER: *Hymenoptera*
SUBORDER: *Apocrita*
SUPERFAMILY: *Scolioidea*
FAMILY: *Formicidae*
SUBFAMILY: *Formicidae*
TRIBE: *Formicidae*
GENUS: *Myrmoteras forel*
SPECIES: *Myrmoteras undet*

In the above classification system ants are first sorted into the *Animalia* (animal) kingdom, together with humans, birds, and all other animals. The many subcategories under Kingdom are used by scientists to further sort animals based on their characteristics.

For example, animals with a tough outer shell and open body cavity are sorted into the phylum *Arthropoda*. These animals are called arthropods. If an arthropod has six legs it is sorted into the subphylum *Hexopoda* (*hex* is the Latin word for six and *pod* is the Latin word for foot).

The sorting stops with the category *species*. Species are the fundamental units of biological classification. There are over 20,000 different species of ants.

Photo courtesy of Brian Fisher, www.antweb.org

in book 7 of Ovid's great poem, the *Metamorphoses*.

Aeetes

Αιητης

Aeetes (eye-EE-teez) was the king of Colchis and a powerful magician. In Greek mythology Aeetes was the guardian of the Golden Fleece, a sacred ram's fleece made from gold. His mother was Perse, an Oceanid (ocean nymph).

When the Greek hero Jason and his crewmen, the Argonauts, asked Aeetes for the Golden Fleece, he agreed. But before he gave them the sacred treasure, Aeetes asked Jason to perform some nearly impossible tasks: First, Aeetes ordered Jason to yoke together two fire-breathing bulls and use them to plow the field of Ares, the god of war. Next, Jason was to sow that field with dragon's teeth.

Aeetes' daughter, the sorceress Medea, had fallen in love with Jason. She used her magical powers to help him accomplish the tasks.

When Jason returned to claim the Golden Fleece, Aeetes was stunned that Jason had performed all his tasks. Aeetes refused to surrender the Golden Fleece. He left it hanging in a grove of trees, guarded by a fierce dragon. Medea, betraying her father's wishes, helped Jason to steal the Golden Fleece.

See also Colchis; Jason; Medea.

Aegaeon

Αιγαιων

Aegaeon (eye-GAY-ahn) was another name for the giant monster Briareus in Greek mythology.

See Briareus.

Aegeus

Αιγευς

PRONUNCIATION: uh-JEE-uhs
GENDER: Male
CULTURE: Greek
ATTRIBUTES: Steadiness

Aegeus became the king of Athens. His son Theseus killed the monstrous Minotaur. The Aegean Sea is named after him.

Aegeus was a prince. His father was Pandion, the king of Athens. When his father died, Aegeus and his brothers competed for control of the throne. Eventually Aegeus prevailed and became king of Athens.

Aegeus married various women, but was unable to beget children by them. This troubled Aegeus because he wanted a son. In desperation, he traveled to Delphi to ask the oracle what he should do. The oracle advised him to have a child with Aethra, the daughter of the king of Troezen. Aegeus traveled secretly to Troezen, and before long Aethra gave birth to Theseus. Aegeus could not marry Aethra, so Theseus grew up without knowing his father.

Aegeus Leaves a Surprise for His Son

One day Aethra asked Theseus to accompany her on a walk. When the pair came across a large boulder by the side of the road, Aethra challenged Theseus to test his strength by moving the gigantic rock. Without any difficulty Theseus was able to roll the boulder aside. Lying under the boulder were a sword and a pair of golden sandals.

Aethra was thrilled. She knew all along that the sword and sandals were there, waiting to be discovered by Theseus. Before Aegeus left Troezen, he had hidden these items beneath the boulder. He told Aethra that when their son was strong enough to roll the boulder aside, he could claim the sword and sandals and join his father in Athens. Aegeus would then proclaim the boy his rightful heir.

The Sword and Sandals Save Theseus

Theseus was overcome with excitement. He journeyed to Athens, ridding the roads of thieves and bandits as he traveled. But when he arrived at Aegeus's palace, things were not as he had expected.

TRUE OR FALSE?

1. Aegeus was the king of Rome.
2. Aegeus had a son named Theseus.
3. Aegeus left a spear and helmet for his son to find.
4. Aegeus married Minerva.
5. Medea tried to trick Aegeus into killing his son.
6. Aegeus drowned himself because he thought his son was dead.
7. The Aegean Sea was named in honor of Aegeus.

Aegeus (continued)

Aegeus's wife at that time was Medea. She found Theseus threatening. She did not allow Theseus to see his father. Medea convinced Aegeus that Theseus was a dangerous visitor who must be done away with. Aegeus agreed to Medea's plot to poison Theseus.

As Aegeus was handing Theseus a cup of poisoned wine, the young man pulled out the king's sword and golden sandals. Aegeus was stunned. He realized that standing before him was his own son. Aegeus dashed the cup of poisoned wine to the floor. He turned toward Medea and could not control his anger. He drove her from his palace and ordered her exiled from Athens.

Aegeus felt nothing but joy over his son's arrival in Athens. Theseus was Aegeus's rightful heir. But soon he remembered that he had a horrible task ahead.

Aftermath of War with Crete

Years earlier, Athens staged the first Panathenaia festival, which was held in honor of the goddess Athena. King Minos of Crete sent his son Androgeus to Athens for the festival. While there, Androgeus competed in the games, beating the Athenians and winning every event. This made Aegeus, king of Athens, so furious that he had Androgeus killed. When word reached King Minos that Androgeus was dead, he declared war on Athens. Crete is the largest island in the southern Aegean basin. It was the most powerful kingdom in all of Greece and Minos easily won the war.

A Monstrous Appetite That Must Be Fed

King Minos then had the power to force the defeated Aegeus to pay dearly for killing Androgeus. Minos demanded that Aegeus help feed the Minotaur, a monster that was half human and half bull. It had an enormous appetite for human flesh. Minos had trouble finding enough people for the Minotaur to eat, so he demanded that Aegeus send fourteen youths, seven boys

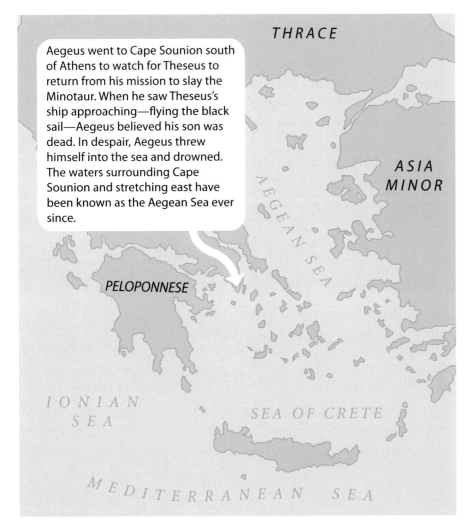

Aegeus went to Cape Sounion south of Athens to watch for Theseus to return from his mission to slay the Minotaur. When he saw Theseus's ship approaching—flying the black sail—Aegeus believed his son was dead. In despair, Aegeus threw himself into the sea and drowned. The waters surrounding Cape Sounion and stretching east have been known as the Aegean Sea ever since.

THRACE

ASIA MINOR

AEGEAN SEA

PELOPONNESE

IONIAN SEA

SEA OF CRETE

MEDITERRANEAN SEA

The Minotaur, a monster that was half human and half bull, had an enormous appetite for human flesh.

and seven girls, to Crete every nine years. The youths would become food for the Minotaur.

Soon after Theseus's arrival in Greece, it was time to send the seven young men and seven young maidens to Crete to be fed to the Minotaur. The brave Theseus asked his father to send him to Crete. Theseus wanted to test his spirit against the Minotaur and become a great hero. Aegeus reluctantly agreed, for he knew that he couldn't hold his brave son back. If Theseus could succeed against the Minotaur, Athens would be free of its terrible nine-year human sacrifice.

Theseus Forgets to Signal Good News

Theseus set sail for Crete on a ship with black sails. He promised Aegeus that if the voyage was successful, he would replace the black sails with white sails. Aegeus would know from a distance that Theseus was returning safely, and that the Minotaur had been conquered.

Theseus was successful in slaying the Minotaur. In his excitement, however, he forgot to change the sails of his ship. When Aegeus saw the ship returning with black sails he thought his son was dead. In his grief Aegeus threw himself into the sea and drowned. He never learned the good news of Theseus's

triumph over the Minotaur. When Aegeus fell into the sea, that body of water was named after him as the Aegean Sea.

FAMILY: Father was Pandion; son was Theseus.

IN ART: Aegeus receiving the oracle of Delphi from the priestess Themis is depicted on a drinking cup displayed in the State Museum of Berlin. The cup was painted by an artist known as the "Kodros Painter" in the fifth century B.C.

MODERN USAGE: The sea where King Aegeus drowned was named the *Aegean Sea* in his honor.

GO TO THE SOURCE: Information on Aegeus can be found in book 3 of the *Library* by Apollodorus. He is also mentioned in Plutarch's *Life of Theseus* and the *Metamorphoses* by Ovid. He also plays a part in the tragic play *Medea* by Euripides.

Aegis

Αεγις

In Greek mythology, the aegis (EE-jihs) was the great breastplate of Zeus, the king of the gods. Hephaestus, the god of fire and blacksmiths, created the aegis for Zeus.

The aegis, believed to be the strongest piece of armor ever cre-

ated, was made of dazzling metal and fringed with tassels of gold. Some Greeks believed the aegis was made from the skin of one of the goats that nursed the infant Zeus. When Zeus shook the aegis, it produced thunder and lightning.

Zeus gave the aegis to his daughter Athena, the goddess of wisdom and warfare. Athena attached the head of the monstrous Gorgon Medusa to the aegis; any mortal who looked directly at Medusa's head was turned to stone. The engraver Nisus created one of the few works of art showing Zeus with the aegis.

See also Athena; Medusa; Perseus; Zeus.

Aegle

Αιγλη

Aegle (EYE-glay) was one of the nymphs known as the Hesperides. In Greek mythology, the Hesperides guarded the sacred garden of the goddess Hera. Growing in Hera's garden was a tree that bore Golden Apples, a wedding gift to Hera from the Earth Mother, Gaea.

See also Erytheis; Hesperia; Gaea; Hera; Heracles; Hercules; Hesperides; Nyx.

Aeneas

Αινειας

PRONUNCIATION: uh-NEE-uhs
GENDER: Male
CULTURE: Greek and Roman
ATTRIBUTES: Destiny; Piety; Loyalty to the national cause

Aeneas was one of the most courageous Trojan warriors who fought in the Trojan War. He and the other Trojan warriors survived many battles and the wrath of the Greek goddess, Hera (Roman Juno). When the Greeks emerged victorious, Aeneas then escaped from Troy and sailed west to Italy. When he arrived there, he fulfilled his destiny by becoming the founder of Rome.

Aeneas was an important hero in both Greek and Roman mythologies. He was the son of Anchises and Aphrodite, the goddess of love. He was born on Mount Ida and grew up in Dardania, a region of Greece. He went on to fight on the side of the Troy in the Trojan War.

When the Trojan War started, Aeneas did not join the battle. However, when Achilles and his men attacked Mount Ida Aeneas led the Dardanians, an army of warriors from his district, into war.

Aeneas and the Dardanians did not arrive in Troy until the ninth year of the Trojan War. But once there, Aeneas became one of the greatest heroes in the Trojan army. Only Hector, the prince of Troy, was braver in battle. But while Hector died at Troy, Aeneas was fated to survive and become the founder of Rome.

Aeneas Fights Bravely, Both as Man and Ghost!

During one of the bloodiest battles of the Trojan War, Aeneas fought one-on-one with the Greek hero Diomedes. Diomedes hurled a large rock at Aeneas, breaking his hip. Aphrodite, often on hand to protect Aeneas from danger, rushed onto the battlefield to help her son. But the aggressive Diomedes wounded her, too, thrusting his spear through her hand. It seemed that Aeneas was doomed!

Then, when all looked lost, the god Apollo swooped in and carried

Aeneas was the son of Aphrodite, the goddess of love. This painting by Giandomenico Tiepolo (1727–1804) is called Farewell of Venus to Aeneas and it shows Aeneas saying goodbye to his mother. Venus tried to protect Aeneas on his many voyages.

TRUE OR FALSE?

1. Aeneas was only important to the Greeks.
2. Aeneas was the son of Aphrodite.
3. Aegeus married Minerva.
4. Aeneas traveled to the Underworld to visit his father.
5. Aeneas married Creusa, Dido, and Lavinia.
6. The descendants of Aeneas founded the city of Athens.
7. There is an opera that tells the story of Aeneas and Dido.

Aeneas (continued)

Aeneas far from the fighting. He took Aeneas to his temple, where he healed the hero's wounds and gave him strength. While Aeneas rested, Apollo created a phantom Aeneas to fight in his place on the battlefield. This ghost fooled both the Greeks and Trojans until Aeneas was ready to return to war.

When Aeneas returned to the fighting, Apollo urged him to fight Achilles, the greatest Greek warrior. Aeneas agreed, but he was no match for Achilles. Just as Aeneas was about to be pierced by Achilles' sword, the sea-god Poseidon rescued him from the battlefield.

Athena, Hera, and the other Olympian gods who favored the Greeks were angry with Poseidon. But Poseidon reminded them that he was only helping Aeneas fulfill his destiny: to become the founder of Rome. All the gods wanted this to come true, for they knew the Romans would become devoted followers of the Olympian gods. Only Hera (Roman Juno) refused to give up her wrath against Aeneas and the Trojans.

Will Aeneas's Family Escape the Burning City of Troy?

Aeneas fought bravely but the Greeks were sacking the city. With Troy lost, Aeneas ordered many Trojan women and children to flee

Aeneas, followed by Ascanius and carrying Anchises from burning Troy.

the city and escape to Mount Ida. Aeneas wanted to continue fighting, and would probably have died at Troy, but the ghost of Hector and his mother Aphrodite both begged him to save himself. He decided to escape.

Aeneas frantically gathered his family together. He found his father, Anchises, who walked with a limp, and lifted the old man onto his shoulders. Aeneas escaped from the burning city, carrying Anchises on his shoulders and holding the hand of his son, Ascanius. (Ascanius was also called by the name Iulus.) Aeneas's wife Creusa followed a few steps behind.

Creusa lost her way during the dangerous journey, but Aeneas did not realize she was missing until he reached Mount Ida. Aeneas ran

back to Troy in search of his beloved wife. As he ran through the burning city, he called her name again and again without success.

Aeneas had given up all hope of finding Creusa when her ghost appeared before him. She told him that she had perished at Troy, and now was an attendant for the goddess Cybele. Weeping for his beloved wife, Aeneas returned to Mount Ida.

Trojans Sail Away to a New Home

On Mount Ida Aeneas assembled all the Trojan survivors. They worked together building ships and planning for a long voyage. Within a year they were ready to sail west to Italy. Aeneas and his followers had faith that the gods would protect them. Under the wise and courageous leadership of Aeneas, the Trojans set sail.

Before long they reached the island of Delos, the birthplace of Aphrodite and the seat of one of Apollo's oracles. The oracle there told Aeneas that the Trojans must seek a home where their race originated. The Trojans believed this land was Crete, the homeland of King Minos and the Minotaur. But there Aeneas was visited by a figure who told him the Trojans needed to leave Crete and sail west.

Monsters, Famine, and Storms in the Way

Aeneas and his men then came to the island of the Harpies. The Harpies were a race of monsters, half woman and half bird. They tore their enemies to shreds using their sharp brass talons. Aeneas and his men angered the Harpies by killing some of their cattle for food. The Harpies flew over the Trojans as they ate, swooping in to steal food and to menace the Trojans. The Trojans were able to fight the Harpies off and to escape, but not before one of the Harpies uttered a curse. She said that before Aeneas could begin building Rome, his people would be struck with a horrible famine. Before the end, the Trojans would be forced to eat their own tables to survive.

After escaping from the Harpies, Aeneas and the Trojans set sail once more, but they were unaware that the goddess Hera was against them. She hated the Trojans and did not want them settling in Italy. Aeneas's ships were on course to reach Italy when Hera called Aeolus, the keeper of the Winds. Hera bribed Aeolus to open the cave where the storm winds were kept locked away. The gales flew out of the cave and caused a terrible storm. The sky turned black and the waves swelled. Aeneas gave up all hope of surviving. But

Aeneas, the founder of Roman civilization, is dressed for battle.

the watchful Poseidon, god of the sea, intervened. Poseidon guided the Trojan fleet to safety on the shores of northern Africa.

Aeneas in Carthage

Aeneas and a few men journeyed inland to explore. They came across Carthage, a great and powerful city. When Dido, queen of Carthage, heard that the hero Aeneas was in Carthage, she welcomed him into her palace. She offered Aeneas and his men food and wine, and Aeneas entertained her with tales from the Trojan War. Before long Aeneas and Dido were deeply in love. After only a few days, Aeneas agreed to marry the queen and share her kingdom.

Aeneas and Dido were so contented that Aeneas forgot about his mission to lead the Trojans to Italy. He lingered in Carthage for many months. Carthage was a growing and prospering city and there was much to keep Aeneas occupied.

Zeus, the most powerful god, looked down from Mount Olympus

Aeneas (continued)

and saw what was happening in Carthage. Zeus dispatched Hermes, the god of travelers and thieves, to talk to Aeneas. Hermes convinced the great hero not to forget his destiny. While Aeneas had deep love for Dido, he realized that he was losing time. It was important for him to return to his mission to establish Rome. One night while the people of Carthage were asleep, Aeneas ordered the Trojans to board their ships. At dawn, Dido discovered that Aeneas was gone. Not wanting to live without Aeneas, Dido used one of his swords to kill herself.

The Trojans Grow Restless

Aeneas and the Trojans sailed from Carthage to the island of Sicily. There, the king welcomed them. The goddess Hera, still angry with the Trojans, sent her messenger, Iris, to turn the Trojan women against the men. Iris convinced the women that their wandering would never come to an end, and that they needed to find a way to keep the men in Sicily. Iris gave the women flaming torches, which they used to set fire to their ships. Aeneas prayed to Zeus for guidance and help. Zeus sent a storm to put out the fires.

Aeneas did not know what to do. His people were growing more and more weary, and many wanted to stay in Sicily. One night, the ghost of his father, Anchises, appeared to Aeneas in a dream. Anchises warned his son of the dangers he faced and urged Aeneas to travel to the Underworld to meet with him.

Aeneas managed to lead the Trojans to Italy. As soon as they arrived, Aeneas sought the cave of the Sibyl. The Sibyl was a woman who could perform magic and predict the future. When Aeneas told the Sibyl of his desire to journey into the Underworld to talk to his father, she agreed to help him. First, Aeneas needed a magical golden bough, which he would find in the forest. Without it, the Sibyl told him, Aeneas would not be able to step into the realm of Hades.

Will Aeneas Find the Way to the Underworld?

Aeneas set out to find the golden branch. At first, he found nothing. Then two doves flew overhead, and Aeneas felt he should follow them. For hours Aeneas walked through the forest, always keeping his eyes on the doves overhead. After many hours, the doves came to rest in a tree. Aeneas was overcome with delight when he saw that the doves were perched on a golden branch. Aeneas raced back to the Sibyl, clutching the branch in his hand.

François Perrier's (1590–1650) painting shows Aeneas and his men fighting the Harpies. The Harpies were creatures with the body of a bird and the head of a woman. They were upset with Aeneas because he and his men had stolen their cattle.

Now the Sibyl could guide Aeneas into the Underworld.

The two began their descent. When Aeneas and the Sibyl reached the banks of the River Styx, at first the ferryman Charon refused to take them across. Only dead souls could cross the Styx. But when Charon saw Aeneas holding the golden branch, he reluctantly agreed to ferry them across the river. Charon's boat, used for ferrying only dead souls, almost sank with the weight of Aeneas, but Charon managed to navigate the river.

Upon entering Hades, Aeneas and the Sibyl soon came to Elysium, a beautiful meadow where the spirits of heroes and noble people lived. It was there that Aeneas found the spirit of his father, Anchises. Anchises urged his son to carry out his destiny to establish Rome. At the same time, Anchises prepared Aeneas for a great war that would take place before his mission could be fulfilled.

The Trojans Reach Italy, Only to Find Trouble

Aeneas left the Underworld and returned to the Trojan camp. He commanded his men to prepare to set sail. Before long, they set sail for Latium, a city on the coast of Italy. Latinus, the king of Latium, welcomed Aeneas and his Trojan followers. He was generous in offering food and drink. At one time, Latinus received a prophecy that his daughter should marry a foreigner. Thinking Aeneas was the foreigner, Latinus offered his daughter, Lavinia, to Aeneas in marriage. Everything seemed peaceful for Aeneas. Then the goddess Hera interfered once again. She sent Alecto, the Fury who directed the devastation and cruelty of war, to Latium.

Alecto first went to Amata, Latinus's wife and queen of Latium. Alecto filled Amata's heart with hate for Aeneas, making her oppose any marriage between him and her daughter. Alecto then went to the nearby kingdom of King Turnus. Years earlier, Latinus had promised Lavinia to Turnus in marriage. When Turnus learned that Lavinia was going to marry Aeneas, he declared war. Latinus could not turn against Amata and Turnus, so Aeneas was on his own, with only a small army at his command.

Without Aeneas, There Would Be No Rome

The war between Aeneas and Turnus could not be avoided. The Trojans proved their valor, fighting off the much larger force. It was clear that the war could only be resolved if Aeneas and Turnus fought each other. Aeneas killed Turnus in one-on-one combat and claimed the hand of Lavinia. He founded the city of Lavinium in her honor. But his destiny was to found Rome, which would take a few more generations. Aeneas's son, Silvius, founded the city of

Aeneas (continued)

Alba Longa, and his descendants built the city of Rome. Many generations later, Romulus, Rome's first king, recognized that Rome would never have existed if it were not for Aeneas.

See also Anchises; Creusa; Dido; Romulus and Remus.

FAMILY: Father was Anchises; mother was Aphrodite, the goddess of love; with his first wife, Creusa, son was Iulus, ancestor of the Julian clan to which Julius Caesar belonged.

IN ART: Aeneas was often depicted carrying his father Anchises on his back or in the company of Queen Dido of Carthage.

Seventeenth-century Italian sculptor Gianlorenzo Bernini produced a marble statue of Aeneas with Anchises and Ascanius in 1618. It is displayed in the Galleria Borghese in Rome.

Giandomenico Tiepolo (1727–1804) painted a picture called *Farewell of Venus to Aeneas* which shows Aeneas saying goodbye to his mother. Venus was the Roman name for Aphrodite.

IN LITERATURE: Interest in the mythology of Aeneas was revived during the Middle Ages, when the hero became the subject of many romances in various languages, including French and Flemish. Aeneas is one of the characters in English poet William Shakespeare's play *Troilus and Cressida.* Shakespeare also refers to Aeneas's romance with Dido in *Hamlet* when Hamlet recalls a performance he has once seen:

> One speech in it
> I chiefly loved: 'twas Aeneas' tale
>   to Dido, and thereabout of it
> especially where he speaks of
>   Priam's slaughter: if it live in
> Your memory, begin at this line; let
>   me see, let me see:
>
>   *Act II scene 2*

Aeneas also appears as a character in the thirteenth-century Italian poet Dante Alighieri's work, *The Inferno.*

IN SPACE: Aeneas is the name of an asteroid located west of the planet Jupiter. Many asteroids near Jupiter are named after Greek and Trojan heroes of the Trojan War.

MODERN USAGE: Composer Henry Purcell (1659–1695) produced the opera *Dido and Aeneas* in 1689. It is based on the Greek myth.

GO TO THE SOURCE: Vergil's *Aeneid* recounts Aeneas's adventures after the Trojan War, leading up to the founding of the Roman race. Aeneas is also found in the *Iliad* of Homer and book 3 of the *Library* by Apollodorus.

Aeolus

Αιολος

PRONUNCIATION: EE-oh-luhs
GENDER: Male
CULTURE: Greek and Roman
ATTRIBUTES: Wind

King Aeolus was the keeper of the four Winds in ancient Greece. He had the power to release the Winds and to calm them as well. Poseidon, god of the sea, often called for the Winds when he created storms.

When Zeus, Greek king of the gods, first became the ruler of the Universe, the Winds were wild and free. They blew and went wherever they pleased. The four Winds were Boreas, the North Wind; Zephyrus, the West Wind; Notus, the South Wind; and Eurus, the East Wind. Zeus knew that the Winds were out of control. He decided to lock them up until they were needed. Zeus and the other Olympian gods

In this painting by the French artist François Boucher (1703–1770) Juno (Greek Hera) is asking Aeolus to release the Winds. The painting hangs in the Kimbell Art Museum in Fort Worth, Texas.

Aeolus (continued)

appointed Aeolus the ruler of the Winds.

King Aeolus lived in a magnificent palace on the floating island of Aeolia. He had only his wife and twelve children—six sons and six daughters—for company. Aeolus kept his home safe from pirates by building a massive wall of bronze around the entire island. Aeolus was well-suited to become keeper of the Winds.

Aeolus was called upon whenever one of the Olympian gods needed one of the Winds. The Winds were kept locked in a cave on Aeolia. Aeolus never allowed more than one Wind to escape at a time.

Poseidon (Roman Neptune), the lord of the sea, called for Aeolus to send Winds more than any other Olympian god. He enjoyed punishing sailors who opposed him, and the Winds were an important ingredient for creating storms. Boreas, the icy-cold North Wind caused many storms. Zephyrus, the West Wind, always blew warmly and softly. Notus, the South Wind, brought rain and fog. Eurus, the East Wind, was the least important of the four brothers.

A Hero Is Blown Off Course

Aeolus played an important role in the myth of the Greek hero Odysseus. On Odysseus's trip

This drawing is of Boreas, the North Wind, as he appears on one of the panels of the Tower of Winds in Athens, Greece, pictured at right.

home after the Trojan War, he came to Aeolia. Aeolus welcomed Odysseus and his men warmly and kept them as his guests for a month. When Odysseus was ready to depart, Aeolus presented him with an ox-hide bag. This was a great gift, for it contained all the Winds except Zephyrus, the soft West Wind. If they kept the unfavorable Winds tied safely in the ox-hide bag, Odysseus and his crew were assured safe passage for their journey home to Ithaca.

For nine days and nights, Odysseus's ships sailed on calm seas, with Odysseus at the wheel the entire time. However, on the tenth day, Odysseus fell asleep. His men, curious to discover what silver and gold Aeolus had given Odysseus, opened the ox-hide bag. The ships at that moment were within sight of Ithaca, but when all the Winds rushed out, Odysseus's ships were blown all the way back to Aeolia. Aeolus, believing that the gods had intervened to cause Odysseus's troubles, sent Odysseus away without any further help.

Aeolus Causes a Storm, but Poseidon Calms the Seas

Aeolus also played a role in the voyages of the Trojan hero Aeneas. When Aeneas sailed west after the Trojan War ended, the goddess Hera (Roman Juno) wanted to interfere with his journey to Italy. She convinced Aeolus to release the Winds and cause a storm. During the terrible storm, Aeneas

and his Winds in two of his plays, *Henry VI Part 2* and *Pericles*.

IN SPACE: Eole, French for Aeolus, was the name of an experimental weather satellite launched in 1971.

MODERN USAGE: An Aeolian harp was a three-foot-long instrument that was often placed on a window ledge so that the wind could catch it and cause its strings to vibrate. It was popular from the late sixteenth century until the late nineteenth century and is now made as a toy.

GO TO THE SOURCE: Aeolus was written about in book 10 of Homer's *Odyssey* and in book 1 of Vergil's *Aeneid*.

felt there was no hope of surviving, but he and his ships were saved when Poseidon took pity on him and calmed the seas.

See also Eos; Odysseus; Aeneas.

FAMILY: Father was Hippotes; mother was Melanippe, a daughter of the Centaur Chiron.

IN ART: The eighteenth-century French artist François Boucher created a large painting entitled *Juno Asking Aeolus to Release the Winds* in 1769. It hangs in the Kimbell Art Museum in Fort Worth, Texas. The Greeks know Juno as Hera.

Aeolus is often represented in art as a healthy man supporting himself in the air by wings.

IN LITERATURE: Jonathan Swift's satire entitled *A Tale of a Tub* contains Aeolists, a fictional religious sect who obtain inspiration from Aeolus and his Winds. William Shakespeare mentions Aeolus

Aesacus

Αισακος

Aesacus (EE-sah-kuhs) was one of the fifty sons of Priam, the king of Troy. Aesacus fell in love with the

Aesacus (continued)

nymph Hesperia. One day, Aesacus pursued Hesperia to make her his wife. As Hesperia ran away, she was attacked by a snake and died from the snakebite.

Aesacus, heartbroken, threw himself into the sea. He was rescued by a sea nymph named Thetis, who changed him into a seabird called the cormorant.

See also Hesperia.

Aeschylus

Αισχυλος

Aeschylus (525–456 B.C.) was not a mythological figure. He was a Greek author of tragedies. He was born in Eleusis in Attica. His father, Euphorion, made sure that Aeschylus participated in religious studies, which later affected the tone of his dramatic works.

The plays of Aeschylus were performed throughout Greece in outdoor theaters like the one pictured here.

In 499 B.C., Aeschylus entered his first competition for the prize offered annually at Athens to the poet producing the best tragedy. It was not until 484 B.C. that he achieved his first victory. In the course of 40 years, he competed nearly 20 times and won first prize in 13 of those competitions. Each time, his contest entry included a collection of three related tragedies followed by a satyr play, or a comic parody.

Before the days of Aeschylus, Greek tragedy consisted of dramas that were acted out by a chorus, a chorus leader, and one actor. There was little plot and no scenery or other accessories. In his plays, Aeschylus added a second actor and invented costumes, including mask, mantle, and the so-called tragic boot. He had the plays produced on a regular stage and used the services of the scene painter. He also gave to Greek tragedy its characteristic literary form. Because of these innovations, he was called the Father of Tragedy.

Aeschylus was serious, bold, and often sublime in style and originality of phrase. In his works, he upheld a reverence for the gods, the sanctity of oaths, the duties of hospitality, and the unbreakable bond of marriage. His plays had simple plots and his heroes were often depicted as victims of destiny. It was the struggle against destiny that usually placed the heroes in their tragic situations.

Though he wrote about eighty plays, only seven are still available today: *The Seven against Thebes, The Suppliants, The Persians,*

Aesculapius, the Roman god of healing.

Prometheus Bound, Agamemnon, The Libation Bearers, and *The Eumenides.*

Aesculapius

Aesculapius (eye-skoo-LAH-pee-uhs) was the Roman god of healing. He was known to the Greeks as Asclepius. He was the son of Apollo and served as physician to the Argonauts.

See Asclepius.

Aeson

Αισων

Aeson (EYE-sohn) was the father of the great Greek hero Jason. Aeson was the heir to the throne of Ioleus, king of Thessaly; however, his stepbrother, Pelias, stole the throne from him. While Jason was away on the quest for the Golden Fleece, Pelias tried to murder Aeson. There are many different accounts of the Argonaut expedition. According to most accounts, Aeson committed suicide while Jason was away.

See also Argonauts; Jason.

Aestas

Aestas (EYE-stahs) was the Roman goddess of summer. She wore a crown of wheat shafts and usually held a sickle in her hand. In Roman art, Aestas was often depicted with the deities of the other three seasons: Ver, goddess of spring; Autumnus, god of autumn; and Hiems, goddess of winter.

See also Autumnus; Hiems; Ver.

Agamemnon

Αγαμεμνων

PRONUNCIATION: a-guh-MEHM-nahn
GENDER: Male
CULTURE: Greek
ATTRIBUTES: Royal Power;
Arrogance; Brutality

Agamemnon was the king of Mycenae and commander-in-chief of the Greek forces in the Trojan War. Agamemnon sacrificed his own daughter, Iphigenia, to receive favorable winds for the Greek ships. When Agamemnon returned from the Trojan War, his wife, Clytemnestra, murdered him.

Agamemnon and Menelaus were two brothers from the Greek kingdom of Mycenae. They fought with their cousins Thyestes and Aegisthus over who would control Mycenae, and the cousins won.

Agamemnon and Menelaus fled to Sparta, where King Tyndareus welcomed them. In fact, King Tyndareus was so happy to have Agamemnon and Menelaus in his land that he gave his two daughters to the brothers in marriage. Agamemnon married Clytemnestra and Menelaus married Helen.

Agamemnon and Menelaus were still unhappy about losing control of Mycenae. With Menelaus's help, Agamemnon returned to Mycenae and drove his cousins out. Agamemnon then claimed the throne of Mycenae for himself, and Menelaus returned to Sparta. When King Tyndareus died, Menelaus took over the throne of Sparta.

Agamemnon and Clytemnestra returned to live in Mycenae. Their family grew to include two daughters, Iphigenia and Electra, and a son, Orestes.

Agamemnon wanted a larger kingdom, so he conquered most of the lands surrounding Mycenae and became the most powerful king in all of Greece. Agamemnon and Menelaus ruled their kingdoms happily for years. Then the goddess Aphrodite made a promise to a prince in nearby Troy and the two brothers' lives were changed forever.

Paris Kidnaps Helen and the Greeks Prepare for War

Aphrodite, the goddess of love, made a promise to Paris, a young prince from Troy. Aphrodite told Paris he could marry the most beautiful woman in the world. Everyone agreed that the most beautiful woman was Helen, but there was one problem. Helen was

This funeral mask was found in the royal tombs at Mycenae, the traditional home of Agamemnon. When archaeologist Heinrich Schliemann found the mask he exclaimed "I have gazed upon the face of Agamemnon." It turned out however, that the mask was much older than Agamemnon could have been. Still, the mask is often called the "Mask of Agamemnon," in memory of Mycenae's famous king. It was made around 1500 B.C.

not free to marry Paris because she was already married to Menelaus.

Paris did not let Helen's marriage stop him from planning to marry her himself. He felt he had the right to take Helen as his wife because of Aphrodite's power as a goddess. So Paris traveled to Sparta and kidnapped Helen.

Menelaus was heartbroken and insulted. He could not allow his wife to be taken away. He was ready to leave for Troy to rescue Helen, but he knew he needed help from his powerful brother. He sent a message to Agamemnon, asking for his advice in planning the rescue.

The powerful Agamemnon agreed that Paris's crime could not go unpunished. He ordered all Greek cities to assemble their best warriors to prepare to set sail for Troy.

Agamemnon (continued)

The bravest chieftains from every city in Greece assembled at Argos. Each had ideas about how to bring Helen back to Sparta. Agamemnon was the most powerful king in all of Greece, and he was also a clever negotiator. He gave expensive gifts to the other chieftains to win their support. Before long, Agamemnon became the leader of all the Greek forces. He then ordered the chieftains to go back to their cities to prepare to wage war on Troy.

For two full years the Greeks prepared for war. At last the time came for the warriors to assemble at Aulis on the eastern coast of Greece. The power of the Greek forces was formidable. The harbor was filled with 1,200 ships ready for battle. Agamemnon provided 100 ships himself. This huge fleet and thousands of warriors set sail for Troy on a mission to rescue Helen, the most beautiful woman in the world.

Problems at Sea

The mission did not start well. The ships had just left the harbor and were sailing in the open sea when they were abandoned by the Winds. As the ships bobbed lifelessly on the calm sea, the warriors became impatient and angry.

Then the warriors learned that Agamemnon's actions were the cause of their plight. Just before the Greeks had sailed out of Aulis, Agamemnon had gone hunting. The stag he killed was sacred to Artemis, the goddess of the hunt. Then Agamemnon boasted that he was more skillful at hunting than Artemis.

This insult was too great for Artemis to ignore. She was determined to punish Agamemnon. She asked the Winds to stay away so the seas would be as calm as glass. Thus, the Greek fleet just floated helplessly in the Aegean Sea, with no Winds to fill their sails and carry them to Troy.

Will Agamemnon Dare to Sacrifice His Daughter?

Agamemnon feared that his troops would rise up against him. Not knowing what else to do, he sought help from Calchas, a soothsayer. The news Calchas delivered was horrifying. Calchas said that Artemis would not forgive Agamemnon's insult unless he offered his own daughter as a sacrifice.

At first, Agamemnon could not even consider taking this action. Sacrificing his own daughter was too horrifying to think about. But as the days wore on, Agamemnon

TRUE OR FALSE?

1. Agamemnon and Menelaus were cousins.
2. Agamemnon became the king of Mycenae.
3. Iphigenia and Electra were Agamemnon's sisters.
4. Agamemnon commanded the Greek forces in the Trojan War.
5. Agamemnon angered Artemis by killing her sacred stag.
6. Agamemnon sacrificed his daughter Electra to appease Artemis.
7. Athena saved Agamemnon from Achilles.
8. Agamemnon was murdered by his wife Clytemnestra.

Ancient Greek playwright Euripides wrote about Agamemnon and the Greeks' sacrifice of a deer to win favor with the gods. Here is an artist's vision of Agamemnon, the leader of the Greeks during the Trojan War, burning the deer over a sacrificial fire.

knew he had no choice. He was desperate to save his mission. To remain leader of the Greek troops, he needed to appease Artemis, so Agamemnon sent for his daughter Iphigenia.

Iphigenia received a message from her father, asking her to come to Aulis. Iphigenia thought her father had arranged for her to marry the Greek hero Achilles in Aulis, so she was excited to make the trip. When she arrived, Iphigenia discovered that she had jumped to a wrong conclusion. Her father had made no marriage plans for her, but rather planned to offer her as a sacrifice.

Iphigenia was a brave young woman. She accepted her fate to give her own life to help her father and the Greeks achieve victory over the Trojans. In the version recounted by Aeschylus, Agamemnon actually kills his daughter and thereby brings upon himself the hatred of his wife Clytemnestra.

Agamemnon (continued)

In the version of the myth recounted by Euripides, at the very last moment, just as Iphigenia was about to be killed, Artemis took pity on her. She carried Iphigenia away, leaving a deer in her place. Calchas declared that Artemis would forgive Agamemnon if the Greeks sacrificed the deer and burned the meat over a sacrificial fire. Once this was done, Artemis indeed forgave Agamemnon and allowed the Winds to blow once more. At last the Greek forces were on their way to Troy.

Greeks Battle Bravely

When the Greeks reached Troy, they found a well-fortified city built on the top of a rocky hill. Achieving victory was not going to be easy. For the next nine years the Greeks relentlessly attacked Troy. Neither side—the Greeks nor the Trojans—was able to gain the upper hand.

The Greek forces managed to keep the Trojans inside their walled city and to conquer all the neighboring cities allied with Troy. But these successes were due to the bravery of the Greek warriors and not to Agamemnon's leadership. In the *Iliad,* Homer describes Agamemnon calling for retreat, but his warriors battled on to victory.

Agamemnon Wants Prizes of War

In ancient times, victorious warriors would take the women of the enemy as prizes of war. After one triumph, Agamemnon took Chryseis, the daughter of Chryses, as his prize. Chryses was a priest of Apollo, the god of light and music. When Chryses found his daughter missing, he went to the place where Agamemnon's army was camped. He begged Agamemnon to return Chryseis. The arrogant Agamemnon refused. He was too proud of the Greeks' victory to give up his prize of war.

Chryses was despondent. He prayed to Apollo to take revenge on the Greeks. Apollo heard the prayer, and for nine full days Apollo's golden arrows rained down on the Greeks, causing disease and terrifying the Greek warriors. Once again Agamemnon had a decision to make. He knew he had to give up Chryseis to save his men, so that's what he did.

After Chryseis was returned to her father, Agamemnon's pride suffered. He felt he deserved a prize of war and went in search of another. He decided to take Briseis for his prize of war. Briseis was the handmaiden of Achilles, the greatest warrior in the Greek army.

Achilles did not willingly give Briseis up. Like Agamemnon, he

In this painting by Giambattista Tiepolo (1696–1770), Briseis is presented to Agamemnon. Agamemnon took Briseis from Achilles. In response to the injustice, Achilles stayed in his tent and refused to fight with the Greeks against Troy.

was proud of her as a symbol of his victory in battle. But Agamemnon was the commander and he had the power to take Briseis for himself. Achilles was so angry that he drew his sword to kill Agamemnon. Athena, the goddess of wisdom, caught Achilles by the hair and restrained him, saving Agamemnon's life.

Can Hector Be Stopped?

Athena may have stopped Achilles from killing Agamemnon, but she did not cool his anger. Because he was insulted by Agamemnon, Achilles refused to help the Greeks in battle against the Trojans. Without their greatest warrior, the Greeks had little hope for victory.

Troy's greatest hero was Prince Hector, the older brother of Paris. Without Achilles fighting for the Greeks, Hector and the Trojans appeared to be unstoppable. Discouraged, Agamemnon planned to issue a command to return home, but the Greek hero Odysseus convinced the men to

keep fighting. In the next battle, Agamemnon fought with renewed energy. His sword cut down many Trojan warriors.

Hector then challenged the Greeks to send their best warrior to face him in one-on-one combat. Agamemnon volunteered, but the Greeks chose Ajax instead.

When neither Ajax nor Hector were victorious, the two agreed to stop fighting. Nothing was accomplished and the fierce battle between the Greeks and Trojans resumed. Neither side made much progress.

Greeks Hide Inside a Wooden Horse

The gates of the city of Troy remained closed tight. The Greeks could not overpower the walled city. The Trojans, safe only within the walls, could not drive away the Greeks.

Athena gave the Greeks the help they needed by inspiring them to build a huge, hollow, Wooden Horse. The Greeks left the Wooden Horse on the beach outside Troy with a small band of warriors hidden inside. The rest of the Greeks boarded their ships

and sailed away out of sight. The Trojans were overjoyed, for they thought the Greeks had run away and left the Wooden Horse as a parting gift. The Trojans wheeled the horse inside the city walls and celebrated their victory late into the night with much wine and song.

The Greeks inside the Wooden Horse were careful to remain silent this whole time. They listened as the celebrations died down. When Troy had fallen silent and all the Trojans were at last asleep, the Greek warriors crept quietly out of their hiding place in the belly of

Agamemnon (continued)

the Wooden Horse. The Greeks attacked, overruning Troy from within its walls. The victorious Greeks burned Troy to the ground. The Wooden Horse became known as the Trojan Horse.

After ten long years, the Greeks triumphed at last! Many brave warriors died on both sides, but Agamemnon was among those who survived.

For his final prize of war, Agamemnon received the Trojan princess Cassandra, who was the daughter of King Priam and Queen Hecuba.

The Greeks were ready to return home. Agamemnon sailed back to Mycenae, ready to celebrate the Greek victory with his people.

A Deadly Homecoming

Clytemnestra, Agamemnon's wife, had taken Aegisthus, Agamemnon's cousin, as her lover during the years Agamemnon was away. Clytemnestra would never forgive Agamemnon for sacrificing their daughter Iphigenia. When Agamemnon returned with Cassandra by his side, Clytemnestra seethed with rage and jealousy. She was determined to punish her husband.

Clytemnestra pretended to welcome Agamemnon home, but she took advantage of the first opportunity to take her revenge. With Aegisthus's help, Clytemnestra killed both Agamemnon and Cassandra. Tales of the murder vary: According to Homer's *Odyssey*, Aegisthus invited Agamemnon to a feast and then

The image on this vase from 500 B.C. is of Clytemnestra being restrained by one of Agamemnon's heralds. Clytemnestra and her lover Aegisthus plotted to kill her husband Agamemnon when he returned from the Trojan War.

murdered him at the dining table. In the tragic play *Agamemnon*, Aeschylus wrote that Clytemnestra and Aegisthus killed Agamemnon while he was bathing. Either way, Agamemnon met his end at the hands of his own wife and her lover.

Electra and Orestes, the surviving children of Agamemnon and Clytemnestra, swore to take revenge on their mother for the death of their father. Orestes eventually avenged Agamemnon's death by slaying Clytemnestra.

See also Clytemnestra; Electra; Iphigenia; Orestes.

FAMILY: Father was Atreus; mother was Aerope; brother was Menelaus; wife was Clytemnestra; son was Orestes; daughters were Electra and Iphigenia.

IN ART: According to Homer, of all the Greek heroes in the Trojan War Agamemnon is most like Zeus, king

The Lion's Gate is over the entrance to the remains of a fortified palace at Mycenae, the historical home of King Agamemnon.

of the gods. Ancient Greek artists conveyed this comparison, depicting Agamemnon with a scepter and a crown (called a *diadem*), the most common emblems of royal power.

Agamemnon was shown in a role as the king of all men. In

45

Agamemnon (continued)

one vase painting Agamemnon is depicted in full armor carrying a spear, leading Briseis away from Achilles.

The *Death Mask of Agamemnon,* a distinctive mask made of gold, is on exhibit at the National Archaeological Museum in Athens, Greece. This mask was found in one of the grave circles at Mycenae where Agamemnon supposedly ruled. German archaeologist Heinrich Schliemann named the mask during his excavations at Mycenae in 1876. Agamemnon was probably not the model for the mask, however. The mask has been dated to about 1500 B.C., while most scholars believe the Trojan War took place around 1200 B.C.

There is evidence that royalty once lived at Mycenae. The best example is the Lion's Gate, named for the two lions, symbols of royalty, carved into the stone above the entranceway. The Lion's Gate was once the only entrance to the city.

IN LITERATURE: Agamemnon's status as one of the greatest Greek warriors in the Trojan War is validated by Homer. In book 2 of the *Iliad,* as the Greek army prepares for battle and the generals organize the warriors, Homer compares Agamemnon to the gods themselves:

…and among them went mighty Agamemnon, his face and head looking like Zeus', who delights in thunder, his waist like Ares', and his chest like Poseidon's. As a huge bull stands out over the other cattle as they graze in fields, so magnificent on that day did Zeus make the Son of Atreus stand among the heroes.

> *Homer,* Iliad, *book 2, lines 476–483; translation by Rick M. Newton*

In Homer's *Odyssey,* Odysseus travels to the Underworld to consult the ghost of the blind prophet Tiresias. One of the many dead heroes he encounters is Agamemnon. Odysseus asks him how he died, and Agamemnon sorrowfully tells him of the plot conceived by Clytemnestra and Aegisthus:

Neither did Poseidon destroy me at sea by raising gusty winds and frightful storms, nor did enemy tribes defeat me on dry land. Instead, Aegisthus plotted with my deadly wife to design my fateful end. He invited me to his home and served me a feast, slaughtering me as if I were a fatted calf at the trough.

> *Homer,* Odyssey, *book 11, lines 406–411; translation by Rick M. Newton*

In the Elizabethan age, the English poet William Shakespeare included Agamemnon as a character in his play *Troilus and Cressida.* He is portrayed as a kingly chief commander.

Agamemnon is referenced in *Sweeney Among the Nightingales* by the twentieth-century poet T. S. Eliot:

The host with someone indistinct
Converses at the door apart,
The nightingales are singing near
The Convent of the Sacred Heart,
And sang within the bloody wood
When Agamemnon cried aloud
And let their liquid siftings fall
To stain the stiff dishonoured
   shroud.

GO TO THE SOURCE: Agamemnon appears in scores of ancient Greek texts. Homer's *Iliad* and *Odyssey* are the earliest existing works that include Agamemnon.

Agamemnon also plays a major role in the trilogy, the *Oresteia,* by the ancient tragic playwright Aeschylus. The *Oresteia* is made up of three plays. In the first, *Agamemnon,* the Greek warrior returns to Mycenae and is murdered by Clytemnestra and Aegithus. In the second and third plays, *The Libation Bearers* and the *Eumenides,* his children, Electra and Orestes, plot revenge on their mother, and, in the end, avenge their father by killing her.

The story of Agamemnon can also be found in book 3 of the *Library* and in books 2–6 of the *Epitome.* Both are works by Greek historian and mythologist Apollodorus, who was probably born around 180 B.C., although

> *"…and among them went mighty Agamemnon,*
> *his face and head looking like Zeus', who delights*
> *in thunder, his waist like Ares', and his chest like*
> *Poseidon's."*
>
> —Homer's *Iliad*

some scholars now date him to the second century A.D.

Information on Agamemnon can also be found in the *Historical Library* of Greek historian Diodorus Siculus (late first century B.C.). Only books 1–5 and 11–20 of the 40 books in the original *Historical Library* survive to the modern day.

Another historian, Herodotus (fifth century B.C.) included Agamemnon in his *History*. The Roman poet Ovid (43 B.C.–17 A.D.?) mentions Agamemnon in his narrative poem, *Metamorphoses*.

Agamemnon appears or is mentioned in the tragic plays of Greek playwright Euripides (fifth century B.C.), including *Iphigenia at Aulis, Iphigenia in Tauris, Hecuba,* and *Electra*. Greek play-wright Sophocles (496 B.C.?–406 B.C.) also wrote of Agamemnon in the tragic plays *Ajax, Electra,* and *Philoctetes*.

Aganippe

Αγανιππη

Aganippe (ah-gah-NIH-pay) was a nymph in Greek mythology. Her father was the river-god Ternessus. She lived in a fountain at the foot of Mount Helicon that was sacred to Apollo and the Muses. For this reason, the Muses are sometimes called Aganippides. Many ancient

Greeks believed the water from this fountain had the power to inspire poets.

It was believed that the fountain was created when the winged horse Pegasus stomped the earth with his hooves.

See also Apollo; Muses.

The Aganippe berlandi spider pictured here is commonly known as the Toowoomba trapdoor spider. It was named after Aganippe, a nymph from Greek mythology. These spiders can mostly be found near the city of Toowoomba, which is located in eastern Australia. This is one of the many species of trapdoor spiders in Australia. They are called trapdoor spiders because of their incredible underground burrows. Their nests are highly camouflaged, and are difficult to find if closed.

Aglaia

Αγλαια

Aglaia (ah-GLAH-ee-ah) was one of the three Graces in Greek mythology. Aglaia was the Grace of splendor and brightness; her sisters were Euphrosyne, the Grace of joy, and Thalia, the Grace of good cheer.

The Graces were the daughters of Zeus and the Oceanid (ocean nymph) Eurynome. The Graces were considered to be the goddesses of beauty, charm, and grace, both in nature and in human conduct. The Graces were often associated with the Muses. They were also attendants of the love goddess Aphrodite.

See also Graces.

The three Graces.

Ajax (Greater)

Αιας

PRONUNCIATION: AY-jaks
GENDER: Male
CULTURE: Greek
ATTRIBUTES: Strength; Courage; "The Shield of the Greeks"

Ajax was a great hero in the Trojan War. Ajax, known as *Telamonian Ajax* or *Greater Ajax,* was a large man. He was both strong and courageous, but was not known for his intelligence. Telamonian Ajax and Odysseus fought to see who would win the armor of the Greek hero Achilles. When the prize was awarded to Odysseus, the humiliated Ajax committed suicide.

Ajax, the son of Telamon, was known as *Telamonian Ajax* or *Greater Ajax.* Telamonian Ajax was a great hero in the Trojan War. Only the hero Achilles was a stronger warrior than Telamonian Ajax.

Ajax Competes for Helen

When he was a young man, Telamonian Ajax went to the city of Sparta to compete for the hand of Helen, the most beautiful woman in the world. Helen's adoptive father, King Tyndareus, feared that her suitors would fight over her. The Greek hero Odysseus suggested that each suitor swear an oath to defend Helen, no matter who was chosen to be her husband.

This suggestion pleased Tyndareus, and each suitor swore to defend Helen no matter what. Tyndareus then chose the wise and brave Greek hero Menelaus to be Helen's husband. All of Helen's other suitors kept their oath and honored the marriage.

Ajax left Sparta and became the leader of Salamis, and Menelaus and Helen ruled happily as king and queen of Sparta. Then one fateful day, Paris, a young prince from Troy, kidnapped Helen and carried her back to Troy. Menelaus called upon her former suitors to uphold their oath and fight to regain Helen.

An alliance of Greek kingdoms was formed to win Helen back from the Trojans. Telamonian Ajax was one of the Greek leaders, and he was captain of 12 of the 1,200 ships that sailed across the sea to Troy.

Ajax and Hector Go Head-to-Head

During the Trojan War, Telamonian Ajax repeatedly proved his bravery

The picture painted on this amphora shows Ajax carrying the body of Achilles back from the battlefield. An amphora is a jar with two handles. This one was made around 500 B.C.

on the battlefield. One day Hector, the greatest Trojan warrior, challenged the Greeks to send their bravest fighter against him. Achilles was the greatest Greek warrior, but he was not available. Telamonian Ajax, the next-bravest warrior, was chosen to fight Hector.

Ajax and Hector engaged in fierce fighting that lasted for a full day. They were equally matched and neither could overpower the other. Both Ajax and Hector recognized the other man's strength and agreed to stop fighting. They respectfully exchanged gifts. Ajax gave Hector his massive belt, and he received Hector's sword in return.

Will Ajax Survive the Fighting?

The fighting between the Greeks and the Trojans resumed. As the battles dragged on, Ajax proved his courage many times. When Achilles' closest friend Patroclus was killed, it was Ajax who ran into the midst of battle to retrieve his body. Later, when Paris killed Achilles, Ajax once again risked his own life. As the Trojan warriors aimed their arrows at him, Ajax flew across the battlefield to carry Achilles' body back to the Greek camp.

Once Achilles' body arrived at the Greek camp, the leaders assembled to give Achilles' armor to the bravest warrior. Odysseus and Telamonian Ajax both competed for the armor. In the end the Greek generals awarded the armor to Odysseus. Ajax was angry and humiliated.

Ajax (continued)

Ajax Is Driven Insane

That night, before Ajax could have his revenge, the goddess Athena drove him insane. Ajax was out of his mind and he had the idea to kill all of the Greek generals including Odysseus.

Ajax crept out of his tent, intent on surprising the Greek generals in their sleep. When he saw a flock of sheep, he mistook them in his crazed mind for the generals. In a wild rage, he killed all the sheep. Believing the largest ram of the flock to be Odysseus, Ajax dragged it back to his tent where he violently tortured the ram to death.

Athena then allowed Ajax's sanity to return. When he realized what he had done, Ajax took the sword that Hector had given him and killed himself.

A Noble Burial for a Noble Warrior

Some of the Greek generals, forgetting Ajax's bravery during the Trojan War, wanted to deny him a noble funeral. A noble funeral involved a ceremony to burn the body. But Odysseus stepped forward to persuade the generals that Telamonian Ajax deserved to be honored as a hero.

Years later Odysseus encountered Ajax in the Underworld. Odysseus tried to speak with the ghost of Ajax, but even in the Underworld Ajax's resentment and anger still burned. Ajax turned away from Odysseus without speaking and faded into the shadows.

See also Ajax (Lesser); Odysseus; Hector.

FAMILY: Father was Telamon, the king of Salamis; mother was Perioboea.

IN ART: Ajax was often depicted in armor, ready for battle. He was known especially for his large shield. During the sixth and seventh centuries B.C., many Greek vase paintings show Achilles and Ajax playing dice, a game that was invented during the Trojan War.

IN LITERATURE: Ajax is one of the characters in William Shakespeare's play *Troilus and Cressida*. Shakespeare portrays him as egotistical and stupid. Ajax is also mentioned in several other plays of Shakespeare, including act 4 scene 7 of *Love's Labour's Lost* where the character Berowne cries out:

> By the Lord, this love is as mad as Ajax: it kills sheep; it kills me, I a sheep: well proved again o' my side.

IN SPACE: Ajax is the name of an asteroid near the planet Jupiter. Many of the asteroids surrounding Jupiter are named after the Greek and Trojan warriors.

MODERN USAGE: Ajax is the name of a commercial cleanser, known

TRUE OR FALSE?

1. Ajax was the son of Telamon.
2. Ajax married Helen.
3. Ajax killed Hector in the Trojan War.
4. Ajax was awarded with the armor of Achilles.
5. Athena drove Ajax insane.
6. Ajax was murdered by Odysseus.
7. The blood of Ajax was changed into a flower.
8. Ajax is often pictured wearing armor.

Ajax was one of the Greek heroes during the Trojan War.

for its "strength" and "toughness" in fighting stains. Ajax is also a town in Ontario, Canada.

GO TO THE SOURCE: The heroic feats of Telamonian Ajax are told throughout Homer's epic poem, the *Iliad.* Homer also wrote about Ajax's ghost in book 11 of the *Odyssey.*

The Greek lyric poet Pindar (522?–443 B.C.) wrote about Telamonian Ajax in his work, the *Nemea.* Of the 120 plays written by Sophocles (496–406 B.C.), his *Ajax* is one of the few that survives to modern times. Ajax also appears in book 13 of Ovid's *Metamorphoses.*

Ajax (Lesser)

Αιας

Ajax (AY-jax), the son of Oileus, was known as Lesser Ajax or Ajax of Locris to differentiate him from Ajax, son of Telamon. Lesser Ajax was one of the Greek heroes of the Trojan War. When the Trojan Horse was rolled up to the walled city of Troy, Lesser Ajax was one of the Greek warriors hidden inside.

Lesser Ajax was not as strong or brave as Telamonian Ajax, but he was, nevertheless, a skilled warrior. Both men fought side by side on the battlefield. Lesser Ajax was one of the best spear throwers in the Greek army, and only Achilles could run faster.

After the death of Achilles' closest friend, Patroclus, the Greeks held funeral games in his honor. Lesser Ajax entered the running race. As one of the fastest runners in all of Greece, Lesser Ajax ran

Ajax (continued)

well ahead of the other contestants until the goddess Athena caused him to trip and fall.

Ajax Disgraces the Goddess Athena, and Is Lost at Sea

Lesser Ajax angered the gods with his actions during the Trojan War. As Troy was burning, Lesser Ajax went inside the temple of Athena. The Trojan princess Cassandra was kneeling in prayer in front of a wooden statue of Athena. Lesser Ajax attacked her, grabbing her by the hair and dragging her along the floor. During their struggle, the statue of Athena tumbled to the floor. Lesser Ajax had disgraced Athena's temple with his violence,

Lesser Ajax was one of the best spear throwers in the Greek Army.

and the goddess vowed to take revenge. She asked Zeus, the king of the gods, and Poseidon, the god of the sea, for help.

With the war over, Lesser Ajax and his men set sail for Greece. Zeus aimed a powerful thunderbolt at Ajax's ship, splitting it in two. Ajax's men clung to the remnants of the ship. Ajax foolishly boasted that he had escaped the wrath of the gods as he clung to a rock in the sea. Upon hearing his boast of arrogance, Poseidon then split the rock with his trident and sent Lesser Ajax to his death.

See also Cassandra.

Alcestis

Αλκηστις

Alcestis (al-SEHS-tihs) and her husband Admetus were the queen and king of Thessaly in Greek mythology. Alcestis, the most loyal wife ever to live, was the daughter of Pelias and Anaxibia, who were king and queen of Iolcus.

Apollo, the god of light, music, poetry, and reason, was punished by Zeus, the king of the gods, for having killed the Cyclopes (one-eyed giants). Apollo's sentence was to obey King Admetus for a year.

Admetus became deathly ill. It appeared he would not live long. Apollo asked the gods to spare his mortal master from death. The

gods agreed, but on one condition: that Admetus find someone who was willing to die in his place.

Admetus, trusting that one of his soldiers would give his life for his king, accepted the gods' offer. However, Admetus could not find anyone willing to die in his place. Not even his parents, who were old and had only a short time left to live, were willing to die for their son. Finally his wife, Alcestis, agreed to die in her husband's place. Before long, Alcestis became weak and died. Her life had ended so that her husband could live.

Heracles Saves Alcestis

The hero Heracles arrived in Thessaly soon after Alcestis died. The heartbroken Admetus told Heracles of his loyal wife's sacrifice. Heracles was moved by Admetus's story, and he journeyed to the Underworld to bring Alcestis back to life. Hades, ruler of the Underworld, agreed to release Alcestis to Heracles. She returned to her husband and lived on, forever remembered as the most loyal wife who ever lived.

The Greek playwright Euripides wrote *Alcestis*, a play that tells the story of Alcestis's sacrifice and return to life after death.

See also Admetus.

Alecto

Αλεκτω

Alecto (uh-LEHK-toh) was one of the three Furies. The Furies were also called the Eumenides. Both the Greeks and the Romans knew the Furies as vengeful goddesses who punished criminals who had escaped justice.

Alecto's sisters were Megaera and Tisiphone. Alecto, whose name means "unceasing in anger," oversaw the devastation and cruelty of war. She was often pictured with her head covered with serpents.

See also Furies; Megaera; Tisiphone.

Alecto is often pictured with her head covered with serpents.

When Alectryon fell asleep on guard duty he suffered the wrath of Ares, who turned him into a rooster.

Alectryon

Αλεκτρυων

Alectryon (uh-LEHK-tree-ohn) was a servant of Ares, the Greek god of war.

One night Aphrodite, the goddess of love, visited Ares. Ares wished to keep his love for Aphrodite a secret, and so he asked Alectryon to stand guard at the palace door while they were together.

The night was quiet, however, and Alectryon could not stay awake at his guard post. Before long the young servant was fast asleep. Helios, the sun god, caught Ares and Aphrodite together. Ares punished Alectryon for falling asleep by turning him into a rooster. From that day forward, Alectryon was forced to announce the rising of the Sun.

See also Aphrodite; Ares.

Alexander

Αλεξανδρος

Alexander (al-ehks-AN-dur) was another name for Paris, the son of Priam. The name Alexander means "Defender of Men."

See Paris.

Alpheus

Αλφειος

Alpheus (AL-fee-uhs) was a river god in Greek mythology. He fell in love with Arethusa, a beautiful wood nymph.

One day, Alpheus came upon Arethusa bathing in a stream, and he chased after her. The pair ran

Alpheus (continued)

and ran until they reached Delos, the birthplace of Artemis, goddess of the hunt. Artemis came to Arethusa's rescue and changed her into a fountain.

Alpheus was so in love with Arethusa that he did not want to give up his pursuit. He transformed himself into a river that flowed beneath the ocean from Greece to Delos. The waters of the river Alpheus joined the fountain of Arethusa, and Alpheus was happy at last. The Alpheus River, which flows through modern-day Greece, carries his name.

As one of his 12 labors, Heracles turned the course of the Alpheus River to clean the Augean stables.

The Alpheus River is located in the Pelopponese (southern Greece), near the site of ancient Olympia, birthplace of the Olympic Games. It is the longest river in the Pelopponese.

See also Arethusa; Heracles.

Althaea
Αλθαια

Althaea (al-THEE-uh) was once the queen of Calydon in Greek mythology. Althaea's husband was King Oeneus, and their son was Meleager.

When Meleager was born, the Fates came to Althaea with a prophecy: They said that Meleager's life would end when the log that was burning on the fire completely burned away.

Althaea, thinking she could prevent the prophecy from coming true, pulled the log out of the fire, and extinguished the flames. She locked the log away in a chest. Many years went by, and Meleager grew into a fine young man.

Can Althaea Protect Her Son from the Prophecy?

One day, King Oeneus angered the goddess Artemis when he failed to make a proper sacrifice to her. As punishment, Artemis sent a wild boar to attack the people of Calydon. Meleager and his uncles—all of Althaea's brothers—set out on a quest to kill the boar.

The story of the boar hunt became famous. Ancient Greek storytellers recounted the tale of the Calydonian boar hunt. The hunting party included Atalanta, a girl whom Meleager loved. Atalanta first wounded the boar, but Meleager came in to kill it. As a

Even though it only grows to about two inches long, the Big-claw Snapping Shrimp is one of the most interesting predators in the ocean. The scientific name for these shrimp, Alpheus heterochaelis, *comes from the Greek river god Alpheus. These shrimp, which live in shallow tropical waters, are unique because of their oversized claws. These claws can grow as large as half the length of their entire body.*

This double picture of a hollyhock flower is a stereograph. When viewed through a special set of glasses called a stereoscope, a stereograph gives a three-dimensional effect. The hollyhock's scientific name is Althaea rosea, *perhaps inspired by Althaea, queen of Calydon.*

reward, Meleager received the hide of the boar, which he presented to Atalanta.

Meleager's uncles were insulted. They thought they, not Atalanta, should receive the boar's hide. The uncles began to argue with Meleager and a fight broke out. In the violence that followed, Meleager killed all of his uncles. Althaea was furious to learn that her son had killed all of her brothers. Angry and grief-stricken, she was determined to punish Meleager.

Althaea remembered the log she had locked away years before. She dragged the box holding the log into the center of the room and opened the lid. Inside she found the half-burned log, just as she had left it. She lifted the log out of the box in a fit of rage and threw it onto the fire. The flames began to consume the log. Before long the last bit of wood turned to ash and burned out. At that moment Meleager died, just as the Fates had predicted.

When Althaea realized what she had done in anger, she was horrified. She left her home and hanged herself.

See also Meleager.

Amazons

Αμαζονες

PRONUNCIATION: A-muh-zahnz
GENDER: Female
CULTURE: Greek
ATTRIBUTES: Aggressiveness; Wildness

The Amazons were a race of warrior women who lived in a land east of Greece. They loved to fight and hunt. The Amazons were devoted to Ares, the god of war, and Artemis, the goddess of the hunt.

The Amazons were warrior women in Greek mythology. Amazons fought and hunted as well as men did. They lived in their own nation far to the east of Greece. Amazon women were skilled in the arts of war, riding, hunting, and farming. The Amazons were devoted to Ares, the god of war, and Artemis, the goddess of the hunt.

Once a year, the Amazon women would meet with men from a neighboring village, have their children, and leave again. An Amazon daughter was raised to be a warrior. An Amazon son was either sent back to the village of his father or put to death. When Amazon daughters grew into young women, their right breasts

Amazons (continued)

were removed to make it easier to shoot using a bow and arrow.

The Amazons fought often against the Greeks. According to one legend, the Greek hero Theseus kidnapped the Amazon queen, Antiope. (Antiope and Theseus's wife were sisters.) The Amazons were enraged and were thirsty for revenge. When the Amazons charged into Athens to recapture their queen, Theseus and his army defended the city. Theseus succeeded in winning victory over the Amazons.

Heracles and the Amazons

The Amazons also encountered the hero Heracles, the strongest man who ever lived. Heracles had been sentenced to perform 12 difficult labors as punishment for accidentally killing his wife and children. His ninth labor was to retrieve the

The Amazons were women known for their skill in battle.

golden belt of Ares. Hippolyta, the queen of the Amazons, had the golden belt in her possession.

When Heracles arrived in the land of the Amazons, they were dazzled by his strength. The Amazons had never met a man who could match them in strength. Hippolyta offered Heracles the golden belt of Ares. Secretly, she also offered Heracles her own hand in marriage. As Heracles and Hippolyta were preparing to leave, the Amazon women attacked them. They thought Heracles was kidnapping their queen. Heracles managed to fight them off, but he could not save Hippolyta from her savage Amazon followers. She was killed in the fighting, but Heracles escaped with the golden belt of Ares.

Achilles and Penthesilea

Later, the Amazon queen Penthesilea led the Amazons into battle on the side of the Trojans during the Trojan War. Penthesilea fought, one-on-one, against the greatest Greek warrior Achilles. Although Achilles fell in love with the beautiful and powerful Penthesilea the moment he first saw her in battle, he was bound to fight her to the death. After he mortally wounded Penthesilea, Achilles held her, soothing her during her last moments of life.

FAMILY: The Amazons were said to be descended from Ares, the god of war.

IN ART: Greek vases and relief sculptures often depicted the Amazons riding into war on horseback. In sculpture and vases from early Greek history, the Amazons were usually dressed just like male Greek warriors, but with one breast exposed. In works of art produced after the Persian Wars (499–448 B.C.) they were usually shown wearing eastern-style caps and pants.

IN LITERATURE: *The Firebrand,* a fantasy novel by twentieth-century writer Marion Zimmer Bradley, features the Amazons and other women of the Trojan War. The Elizabethan playwright William Shakespeare used the term *Amazon* to refer to women who took part in war in several of his plays including *King John, Coriolanus, Timon of Athens, Henry VI part I,* and *Henry VI part III.*

In book 9 of the epic poem *Paradise Lost,* English poet John Milton described the leaves that Adam and Eve use to cover themselves as being "broad as Amazonian targe." A targe is a type of shield.

MODERN USAGE: The term *amazon* is used in reference to a woman

who is large in stature, physically powerful, and strong-willed.

The Amazon River is the second-longest river in the world (at about 4,000 miles/6,400 kilometers). It flows in South America. Spanish explorers claimed they saw tribes of large women along its banks, and named the river for the Amazons of Greek mythology.

GO TO THE SOURCE: Information about the Amazons can be found in the *Library* by Apollodorus, book 2, chapter 5. Other information can be found throughout Pausanias's *Description of Greece.*

This advertisement for a hair product that the maker claimed would make hair grow longer and thicker is from the 1860s. Names and terms from Greek and Roman mythology are frequently used to name commercial products.

Ambrosia

Αμβροσια

Ambrosia (am-BROH-zhuh) was the food of the Greek gods and was thought to preserve their immortality. The ancient Greeks believed that ambrosia may have been a type of purified honey. The ancients believed that ambrosia, placed in the wounds of a dead body, could keep the body from decaying. In modern times, ambrosia describes anything that tastes or smells especially good. A modern recipe for ambrosia calls for oranges and coconut.

See also Nectar.

Amor

Amor (AH-mawr) was another name for the god known to the Greeks as Eros and to the Romans as Cupid. The name Amor is also the Latin word for "love." The adjectives enamored ("to be in love with") and amorous ("to be motivated by love") come from his name. *See* Cupid; Eros.

Amphion

Αμφιων

PRONUNCIATION: AM-fee-awn
GENDER: Male
CULTURE: Greek
ATTRIBUTES: Music

Amphion was one of the greatest musicians in the world, second only to Orpheus in skill. Amphion and his brother started to build a wall around the city of Thebes. When Amphion created beautiful music with his lyre, the stones moved into place on their own.

Amphion and his twin brother Zethus were the sons of Zeus and Antiope. The boys were born on Mount Cithaeron, but they were left on the mountain to be raised by shepherds.

The two boys were unaware that their father was Zeus, king of the gods, until they were grown men. Of the two, Zethus was the stronger and more skilled in hunting. Amphion was gentler and less interested in war or hunting. Hermes, the god of shepherds and travelers, visited young Amphion and gave him a *lyre,* which is a type of harp. Amphion learned quickly and mastered the instrument. It wasn't long before Amphion was known as one of the greatest musicians in the world.

Years later, when Amphion and Zethus were grown men, they heard a knock on their door. When they opened it, a woman was standing before them asking for help. When they asked her name, her response stunned them. The woman on their doorstep was Antiope, their mother!

A Lost Mother's Story

Antiope told her sons this story: Years earlier, Antiope was married to King Lycus of Thebes when she became pregnant with a child by Zeus, king of the gods. Lycus was furious, and he turned away from Antiope and married Dirce. Dirce, a cruel woman, was jealous of Antiope and ordered her put in chains.

After many years of horrible slavery, Antiope was finally able to escape. She fled Thebes and went searching for her twin sons, Amphion and Zethus.

Amphion and Zethus had not known that they were sons of Zeus. But now that they had discovered the cruelty their mother had endured, it was their duty to take revenge on Lycus and Dirce.

The two brothers assembled a small army and marched against Thebes. Lycus was killed in the fighting, but the brothers managed to capture Dirce. Because of her cruelty to Antiope, Amphion and Zethus wanted to punish Dirce. They tied Dirce to the horns of a

TRUE OR FALSE?

1. Amphion and Zethus were brothers.
2. Amphion and Zethus were raised by wolves.
3. Amphion was known as a great musician.
4. Amphion and Zethus became rulers of Rome.
5. Amphion built a wall by playing on his lyre.
6. Amphion married Niobe.
7. Amphion had 14 children.
8. Apollo killed Amphion.

Amphion was given a beautiful lyre (a musical instrument similar to a harp) by the god Hermes. Amphion's beautiful music caused the walls of Thebes to build themselves.

tion of the wall. Zethus was not even halfway done. Zethus could not believe that his brother had accomplished so much using only the power of music.

Niobe, A Foolish Queen

Soon after that, Amphion took beautiful Niobe to be his wife. They lived happily together for many years, surrounded by seven beautiful daughters and seven handsome sons.

But Niobe proved to be a foolish queen. Niobe told the people of Thebes that the goddess Leto was not worthy of their worship since Leto had only two children, the twin gods Artemis and Apollo, while Niobe had fourteen. When Artemis and Apollo learned of this insult, they went to Earth and shot all fourteen of Niobe's children with their arrows.

Amphion, overcome with grief over the deaths of his children, fell on his own sword, killing himself.

See also Apollo; Artemis; Niobe; Zethus.

FAMILY: Son of Zeus and Antiope; twin brother of Zethus.

bull by her hair and allowed the bull to drag Dirce around Thebes until she was dead.

The Walls of Thebes

The people of Thebes were happy to be rid of their cruel king and queen. Amphion and Zethus became the kings of Thebes. To protect their new kingdom, the brothers began to build a massive wall to surround the city.

The strong Zethus challenged his brother Amphion to a contest to see who could build faster.

Zethus, confident that he would win, went straight to work stacking gigantic stones, one on top of the other. Amphion had a different plan. He picked up his lyre and started to play. The music drifting forth from the lyre was so beautiful and magical that the stones began to move themselves. Before long, Amphion had completed his sec-

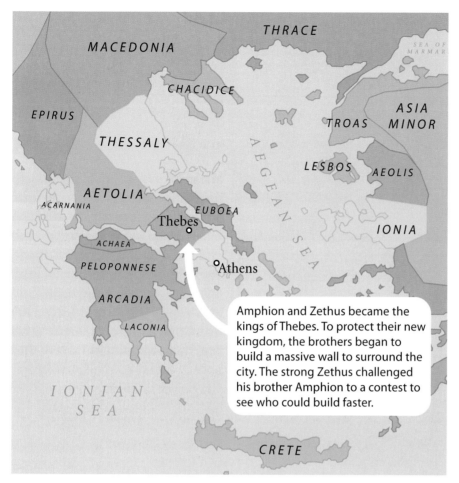

Amphion and Zethus became the kings of Thebes. To protect their new kingdom, the brothers began to build a massive wall to surround the city. The strong Zethus challenged his brother Amphion to a contest to see who could build faster.

IN ART: The French artist Marie Louise Elisabeth Vigée-Lebrun (1755–1842) produced a painting, *Amphion Jouant de la Lyre* (Amphion Playing the Lyre). This work shows Amphion using the power of music over the Naiads and nature.

Two Greek sculptors—Apollonius of Tralles and his brother Tauriscus—are believed to have created a sculpture, *Farnese Bull,* depicting Amphion and Zethus punishing Dirce, in the first or second century B.C. In the sculpture, the brothers are tying Dirce by the hair to the horns of the bull. A Roman copy of the sculpture was made a decade later and may now be seen in the National Museum in Naples, Italy.

IN LITERATURE: The power of Amphion's lyre is often referred to in poetry. Most notable is Alfred Lord Tennyson's poem *Amphion:*

> O, had I lived when song was great
> In days of old Amphion,
> And ta'en my fiddle to the gate,
> Nor cared for seed or scion!
> And had I lived when song was
>   great,
> And legs of trees were limber,
> And ta'en my fiddle to the gate,
> And fiddled in the timber!

William Shakespeare referred to Amphion raising the walls of Thebes when his character Sebastian in *The Tempest* said:

> His word is more than the
>   miraculous harp;
> He hath raised the wall and houses
>   too.

IN SCIENCE: NASA's *Amphion Project* uses artificial intelligence to apply the many different computer software programs developed by NASA scientists to specific problems.

GO TO THE SOURCE: The ancient Greek writer Apollodorus described the building of the wall around Thebes and Amphion's marriage to Niobe in book 3, chapter 5 of his major work, the *Library.* Homer mentioned Amphion in book 24 of the *Iliad* and in book 11 of the *Odyssey.*

Amphion is also mentioned in *Seven Against Thebes,* a tragic play by Aeschylus; and in *Phoenician Women,* a tragic play by Euripides.

Roman authors also wrote of Amphion. In book 6 of the poem, *Metamorphoses,* the Roman poet Ovid mentioned Amphion in his account of Niobe.

Ancaeus

Αγκαιος

Ancaeus (ahn-KY-us) was the son of Poseidon, the Greek god of the sea. Ancaeus was the helmsman on the *Argo* and accompanied the hero Jason on his quest for the Golden Fleece.

Ancaeus planted a vineyard so that he could produce his own

wine. However, a soothsayer warned Ancaeus that he would not live to taste the wine from his grapes. Ancaeus did not believe the soothsayer, and as soon as his first grapes were ripe, he squeezed some of their juice into a cup. Just as he was about to drink, he received word that a wild boar was attacking his lands. Before taking a sip, Ancaeus put down the cup and went off to hunt the boar. Ancaeus was killed by the beast before he could taste his wine. From this story comes the proverb, "There's many a slip 'twixt the cup and the lip."

See also Argo; Jason.

Anchises

Αγχισης

Anchises (an-KY-zeez) was the king of Dardanus and an ally of Troy during the Trojan War. He was the son of Capys and Themis, who was the goddess of law and justice.

One day, Aphrodite, the goddess of love, noticed the handsome Anchises. She went to Earth disguised as a mortal, and soon they were lovers. Before she left for Mount Olympus, Aphrodite warned Anchises not to brag that he was the husband of a goddess. Anchises agreed, and he kept his word for many years—but he could

not keep his marriage a secret forever. When Zeus discovered that Anchises had broken his promise, he threw a lightning bolt at the poor king. Anchises walked with a limp from then on.

Anchises and His Son Aeneas

Anchises and Aphrodite had a son, Aeneas, one of the best Trojan warriors and the founder of Rome. Anchises was too old to fight in the war, but Aeneas proved his bravery many times. After the Greeks succeeded in capturing Troy, Aeneas and Anchises were among the only Trojan survivors. As Troy burned, Aeneas escaped the city, carrying Anchises on his shoulders.

See also Aeneas; Aphrodite.

Andromache

Ανδρομαχη

PRONUNCIATION: an-DRAW-muh-kee
GENDER: Female
CULTURE: Greek
ATTRIBUTES: Dedication

Andromache was the wife of Hector, Troy's greatest hero during the Trojan War. She begged her husband not to go into battle. Her fear that Hector would die became reality. Hector was killed by the Greek hero Achilles.

Andromache was a faithful and loving wife. Her husband was Hector, Troy's greatest hero during the Trojan War.

TRUE OR FALSE?

1. Andromache was married to Hector.
2. Apollo killed Andromache's father and brothers.
3. Andromache was pleased that Hector went to war.
4. Andromache had two sons, Astyanax and Pergamus.
5. There was once a shrine to Andromache in Pergamum.
6. There is a species of bird named for Andromache.

Andromache (continued)

Early in the Trojan War, Andromache learned a harsh lesson about the Greek warrior Achilles. During a battle, Achilles killed Andromache's father and her seven brothers. She was heartbroken. From that day forward, whenever Andromache heard Achilles' name, she trembled with fear. She knew better than any Trojan warrior how dangerous Achilles was.

Is This Hector's Last Visit to Troy?

As the Trojan War wore on year after year, a fight between Hector, the leader of the Trojan forces, and Achilles, the greatest Greek warrior, seemed certain. One day, after the fighting had been raging for months and years, Hector retreated from the battlefield. He entered the walled city of Troy and asked to see his wife Andromache and their infant son Astyanax. Meanwhile, Andromache herself had left her house to see if she could see Hector on the battlefield from the walls of Troy.

Hector and Andromache met on the walkway that topped the walls of Troy. Andromache could see the fighting below. Fearful of what would happen, she begged Hector not to return to the battle. Hector held his wife and tried to comfort her. He reminded her that the Trojans had little chance of victory without him as their leader. Hector hugged his wife and kissed the forehead of his infant son Astyanax.

French artist Jacques Louis David (1748–1825) depicted Andromache and her son, Astyanax, mourning Hector, who died in one-on-one combat with the Greek hero Achilles. Hector's war helmet and sword lie near the bed. This large work is displayed in the Louvre Museum in Paris, France.

"My beloved husband, your courage will be the death of you. You have no pity for your infant son or for luckless me, who will soon be your widow..."

— Andromache addressing Hector in Homer's *Iliad*

When Hector went back to fighting, Andromache's heart sank. She knew that Hector would soon face Achilles in battle. Hector was the Trojans' bravest warrior, but Andromache knew he was no match for the fierce Greek warrior. Andromache turned away from the battlefield and began to prepare herself to mourn her husband's death.

A Wife Will Know Only Grief

When the heroes Hector and Achilles finally met on the battlefield, Andromache's fear was fulfilled. Achilles brutally murdered Hector and then tied Hector's lifeless body to his chariot and dragged it around and around the walls of Troy. After that, it was not long before the Trojan War ended with the Greeks victorious.

In victory, the Greeks were cruel to the defeated Trojans. They did not make an exception for Hector's wife Andromache. She became the property of Neoptolemus, the son of Achilles, as a prize of war. The Greeks took Astyanax from his mother's arms and threw him over the walls of Troy.

After the war Neoptolemus took Andromache to his home in Epirus against her will. There, she lived unhappily as his wife, and became the mother of three children with him. After Neoptolemus died, Andromache then married Hector's brother Helenus. Helenus then became the king of Epirus.

When Helenus later died, Andromache returned to Asia Minor with her youngest son, Pergamus. Pergamus became the founder of a great city, Pergamum. In ancient times, there was a shrine in Pergamum dedicated to the memory of Andromache. The modern town of Bergama in western Turkey lies near the ruins of ancient Pergamum.

FAMILY: Daughter of Eetion; wife of Hector, Neoptolemus, and Helenus; mother of Astyanax and Pergamus.

IN ART: The scene where Andromache is trying to convince Hector not to go into battle was often depicted by artists in ancient times. French painter Jacques Louis David created *Andromache Mourning Hector,* in 1783. A large work measuring 6'8" by 9'10", the work shows Andromache sitting beside Hector's dead body, with her son standing next to her. It hangs in the Louvre Museum in Paris, France.

IN LITERATURE: A famous passage in Homer's epic, the *Iliad,* recounts the scene where Andromache pleads with Hector not to leave for battle. Homer describes the scene where Andromache is holding their son, Astyanax, in her arms:

> Hector smiled in silence as he looked upon his son. Andromache stood next to him, shedding a tear. She took her husband by the hand and said to him, "My beloved husband, your courage will be the death of you. You have no pity for your infant son or for luckless me, who will soon be your widow...It would be better for me to die if I were to lose you, since I have no other comfort in life once you go to your fate. I will know only grief."
>
> *Homer,* Iliad, *book 6, lines 404–413; translation by Rick M. Newton*

IN SCIENCE: *Catocala andromache* is the name of a species of moth. These moths, found in the Southwest United States, feed on the leaves of trees, mostly oaks.

GO TO THE SOURCE: Andromache appears in numerous ancient works, often begging Hector not to fight Achilles. This famous scene can be found in book 6 of Homer's great epic poem, the *Iliad*.

The Athenian tragic playwright Euripides also wrote a play about her, the *Andromache*. Additional information on Andromache can be found in the *Epitome* of the Greek historian Apollodorus.

Andromeda

Ανδρομεδη

PRONUNCIATION: an-DRAW-meh-duh
GENDER: Female
CULTURE: Greek

Andromeda was an Ethiopian princess. Her mother angered the god of the sea, Poseidon. He punished Ethiopia by sending floods and a sea monster. To win Poseidon's forgiveness, Andromeda was offered as a sacrifice to the sea monster. She was rescued by the hero Perseus.

Andromeda was a beautiful princess. Her parents were King Cepheus and Queen Cassiopeia of Ethiopia.

Her mother, Queen Cassiopeia, boasted that Andromeda was more beautiful than the Nereids (sea nymphs). This claim infuriated Poseidon, god of the sea. No mortal could claim to be more beautiful than the gods!

Poseidon's Punishment

To punish Cassiopeia, Poseidon sent damaging floods to Ethiopia. He also sent a sea monster to the waters near Ethiopia. The sea monster sank every ship that entered Ethiopia's waters. Countless sailors perished.

Cepheus, the Ethiopian king, did not know what to do. He could not allow all his people to die at sea. Cepheus prayed to the Egyptian god Ammon, asking for guidance on how to stop the monster. Ammon promised that if Cepheus sacrificed Andromeda to the sea monster, the monster would be satisfied and Ethiopia's waters would again be safe. With a heavy heart, Cepheus knew what he had to do.

Will Andromeda Survive?

Cepheus told his servants to chain Andromeda to a rock on the shore of the sea, where the sea monster could reach her. The hungry sea monster emerged from the water and saw Andromeda, who was struggling to free herself. The huge monster moved through the water toward the rock where Andromeda was chained. His jaws were opening to swallow her just as the hero Perseus flew overhead on his winged sandals.

Perseus swooped down to help Andromeda. He thrust his curved sword into the monster's throat, killing it with a single stroke. Perseus then freed Andromeda from the rock and took her for his wife.

When Andromeda and Perseus returned to the royal palace of Cepheus, their wedding plans were interrupted. Cepheus had promised his brother Phineus that he

TRUE OR FALSE?

1. Andromeda was the princess of Eritrea.
2. Andromeda was the daughter of Cassiopeia and Cepheus.
3. Cepheus chained Andromeda to a large rock by the sea.
4. Perseus rescued Andromeda from a lion.
5. Athena changed Andromeda into a constellation.
6. Andromeda is also the name of a galaxy.

could marry Andromeda. Phineus and his men were waiting at the royal palace, ready to fight for Andromeda's hand. Perseus won the battle with the help of the head of Medusa, which Perseus carried in his magic bag.

Andromeda and Perseus were wed, and they returned to Seriphus, Perseus's homeland. The two lived happily there for the rest of their lives. When Andromeda eventually died after a long and happy life, she was placed in the heavens as a constellation.

FAMILY: Father was Cepheus, king of Ethiopia; mother was Cassiopeia.

IN ART: Ancient Greek vase paintings often depicted Andromeda being prepared for sacrifice to the sea monster, or being rescued by Perseus. In one vase painting, two servants support Andromeda while three others prepare the stakes to which she was to be tied. King Cepheus and Perseus watch, and look miserable at the sight. This vase may be viewed at the British Museum in London, England.

A vase painting from a fourth-century *amphora* depicts Andromeda with her arms outstretched. (An amphora is a Greek vase with two handles near the neck.) Just below, Perseus battles with the sea monster.

Many modern artists have painted the scene of Andromeda chained to the rock, with Perseus nearby. Some of these paintings depict Perseus on the winged horse Pegasus, which sprang from Medusa's neck. Others simply depict Andromeda herself, with only a glimpse that Perseus is nearby. In the 1640s, Flemish painter Peter Paul Rubens made several paintings of Andromeda, depicting her both with and without Perseus.

In Lord Frederic Leighton's painting *Perseus and Andromeda,* the sea monster looks more like a dragon. Andromeda is in chains, and the dragon's wing creates a shelter above her. Perseus appears

Andromeda (continued)

at the top of the painting, bathed in golden light. The hero resembles a god as he descends on the back of Pegasus.

IN LITERATURE: Ovid, in his work the *Metamorphoses,* wrote of the first encounter between Perseus and Andromeda. Ovid captures the fear that must have gripped Andromeda at that moment:

> As soon as Perseus saw her there bound by the arms to a rough cliff—save that her hair gently stirred in the breeze, and the warm tears were trickling down her cheeks, he would have thought her a marble statue.
>
> Smitten by the sight of her exquisite beauty, he almost forgot to move his wings in the air. Then, when he alighted near the maiden, he said: "Oh! those are not the chains you deserve to wear, but rather those that link fond lovers together! Tell me your country's name and yours, and why you are chained here."
>
> She was silent at first, for, being a maid, she did not dare address a man; she would have hidden her face modestly with her hands but that her hands were bound. Her eyes were free, and these filled with rising tears.
>
> *Ovid, Metamorphoses, book 4, lines 673–686; translation by Frank Justus Miller*

Andromeda, chained to the rock, is mentioned in the poem, *On the Sonnet,* by nineteenth-century English poet John Keats. Keats draws a parallel between the Andromeda myth and the constraints placed upon the English sonnet:

> If by dull rhymes our English must
>   be chained,
> And, like Andromeda, the Sonnet
>   sweet
> Fettered, in spite of pained
>   loveliness

IN SPACE: After Andromeda's death, Athena placed her among the stars, forming a constellation in the Northern Hemisphere. She is seen with her arms extended and chained, commemorating the moment of her rescue by Perseus. The Andromeda constellation's brightest star, Alpheratz (Alpha Andromedae), forms the northeast corner of the Square of Pegasus. This constellation also contains the Andromeda Galaxy, the closest large-size galaxy to the Milky Way and the only galaxy in the Northern Hemisphere that is visible to the naked eye. The Andromeda constellation reaches its height in the evening sky during the month of November.

IN SCIENCE: In the system of scientific naming, the genus name *Andromeda* is applied to plants in the heather family that naturally attach themselves to rocks. Plants in this genus can be found in North America, Europe, and Asia. One plant in this genus, *Andromeda polifolia,* commonly known as bog rosemary, can be found growing in British peat bogs. Its flowers are bright pink.

GO TO THE SOURCE: Andromeda's rescue is recounted by Apollodorus in book 2, chapter 4, of the *Library.* For a more detailed account of her rescue and the battle between Perseus and Phineus, consult books 4 and 5 of Ovid's *Metamorphoses.*

Antaeus

Ανταιος

Antaeus (an-TEE-uhs) was a Giant and the son of the Greek Earth Mother, Gaea. Antaeus's strength was invincible as long as he remained in contact with his mother, the Earth. Antaeus challenged all who passed by his hut to wrestle with him. The great hero Heracles was the final person to accept the Giant's challenge. As the two grappled, Heracles appeared to be winning. But whenever Heracles threw Antaeus to the ground, he sprang up again, fully revived. Heracles soon realized that Antaeus could not be defeated as long as he touched the Earth. Heracles seized Antaeus, lifted him above his head, and squeezed the life out of him.

See also Gaea; Heracles; Hercules.

Andromeda: The Princess

Andromeda is seen with her arms extended and chained, commemorating the moment just before her rescue by Perseus. Andromeda is surrounded by many other constellations of important characters in her life. Perseus, the great hero who rescued her, and her parents Cepheus and Cassiopeia are nearby constellations.

The easiest way to recognize this constellation is to first locate the (1) Andromeda Galaxy. This galaxy is a spiral galaxy, and is the largest and brightest galaxy visible from Earth.

The brightest star in Andromeda is (2) Alpheratz, making it the head of Andromeda. This star is about 97 light-years from Earth and is close to 200 times brighter than the Sun. It is a binary star, meaning that it is actually two different stars that orbit around each other. Alpheratz also connects Andromeda to the constellation Pegasus.

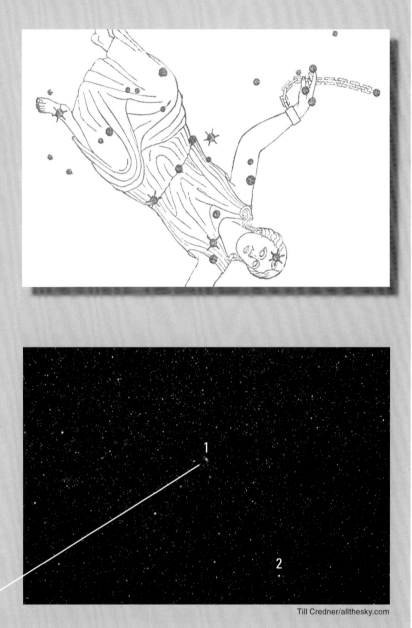

Till Credner/allthesky.com

The Andromeda galaxy is about 2.3 million light-years away, and is traveling toward Earth at a speed of about 84 miles per second. Some scientists predict that Andromeda will collide with our own galaxy, the Milky Way, in about 3 billion years.

Antigone

Αντιγονη

PRONUNCIATION: an-TIH-goh-nee
GENDER: Female
CULTURE: Greek
ATTRIBUTES: Faithfulness; Duty;
    Piety

Antigone was the daughter of the tragic Greek hero, Oedipus. She disobeyed Creon, her uncle, and dared to bury the body of her brother. When Creon found out he was angry. He declared that Antigone should be buried alive as punishment.

Antigone was the daughter of the Greek hero, Oedipus. The story of Oedipus is one of the most tragic in all of Greek mythology.

An oracle told Oedipus's father that he was fated to be killed by his own child. This prediction eventually came true. Without knowing it, Oedipus murdered his father and married his mother. When Oedipus realized that his wife was his mother, he gouged out his own eyes.

He left Thebes, where he was king, to wander aimlessly. Only Antigone and Ismene, his daughters, went with him. Soon after they arrived in Athens, Oedipus died. Antigone and Ismene went back to Thebes.

A Sister's Secret Act

When Antigone arrived in Thebes, she found chaos. Her two brothers, Eteocles and Polynices, had fought over who would inherit the throne of Thebes. Finally, they decided to share the throne, each reigning for one year at a time. However, when his year was up, Eteocles refused to surrender the throne.

A war broke out between the two brothers. In the fighting, both Eteocles and Polynices were killed. With both brothers dead, Creon, their uncle, became king of Thebes. He ordered a regal burial for Eteocles, but declared that no one could bury Polynices.

Antigone could not bear to let Polynices' body remain unburied. She crept out during the night and gave Polynices a secret burial.

She returned to the makeshift grave the very next day at high noon, to ensure that she would be caught. Antigone wanted to defy Creon openly because she believed that his edict was morally wrong: even a king should not overthrow the unwritten laws of Zeus!

Honesty Rewarded with Punishment

Creon was outraged that Antigone had disobeyed his laws. Antigone

TRUE OR FALSE?

1. Antigone was the daughter of Oedipus.
2. Eteocles and Polynices were Antigone's brothers.
3. Antigone was rewarded for giving her brother a proper burial.
4. Antigone was beheaded by her uncle.
5. Haemon loved Antigone.
6. Sophocles and Euripides wrote plays about Antigone.
7. After burying her brother, Antigone went to Carthage to hide from Creon.

Antigone with her father, Oedipus. In the early nineteenth century Austrian historical artist Johann Peter Krafft painted her crying at her father's knee. In 1843 French artist Charles François Jalabert painted the pair being jeered at by citizens of Thebes in his work, *Oedipus and Antigone, or the Plague of Thebes.*

IN LITERATURE: Twentieth-century French playwright Jean Anouilh wrote a play entitled *Antigone.* It updates the tragedy by Sophocles. New translations of *Antigone,* a tragedy by Sophocles, are produced each decade and the play is performed on modern stages throughout the world. A film version of *Antigone* was produced in 1972.

GO TO THE SOURCE: Antigone's story was told by Sophocles in *Antigone* and *Oedipus at Colonus. Antigone* and *Phoenissae* are two plays by the Greek playwright Euripides that survive to the modern day.

told him that his laws were nothing compared to the laws of the gods. She said it was her duty to bury her brother, and that only the gods themselves could stop her from doing so.

In his anger, Creon punished Antigone with a fate worse than death: he ordered her buried alive.

Creon's men took Antigone to a deep underground cave. They pushed Antigone into the cave and blocked the opening. Antigone was trapped with no way to escape.

Soon after, Creon's son Haemon went to the cave to find Antigone. He planned to declare his love for her. When Haemon reached the cave, he cleared away the opening. He rushed in, but found Antigone dead. She had

hanged herself from the rocky ceiling of the cave. Haemon was overcome with grief. Staring at Antigone's lifeless body, Haemon fell on his sword, killing himself.

FAMILY: Father was Oedipus; mother was Jocasta; brothers were Eteocles and Polynices; sister was Ismene.

IN ART: A scene showing Antigone placing Polynices on a funeral pyre was found on a sarcophagus at Rome. A vase from the fourth century B.C. shows Antigone, Eteocles, and a young woman carrying a hydria vessel with three handles at the tomb of Oedipus. This vase is now displayed at the Louvre Museum in Paris, France. Modern painters have depicted

Aphrodite

Αφροδιτη

PRONUNCIATION: af-roh-DY-tee

EQUIVALENT CHARACTER: The Roman
    goddess Venus

GENDER: Female

CULTURE: Greek

ATTRIBUTES: Love; Beauty; Lack of
    self-control

Aphrodite was the goddess of love. She was also the goddess of nature, gardens, and all living creatures. She possessed a magic girdle, a type of belt that granted the wearer the power to inspire love. The dove and swan were two of her favorite birds, so they are often seen in depictions of Aphrodite. Two plants—myrtle and rose—are also associated with Aphrodite. Other symbols of the goddess include the tortoise, ram, and dolphin.

The downfall of Uranus, the first divine king of the Universe, was the cause of Aphrodite's birth. Long before Zeus and the other Olympian gods ruled over the Universe, the Titan Cronus rose up against his father Uranus. After defeating him, he cut up Uranus's body and threw the pieces into the ocean. The flesh of Uranus's body gave off a white foam, and it was from this foam that Aphrodite was born.

When she arose from the water, Zephyrus, the West Wind, gently blew her to the island of Cyprus. Tradition also maintains that she was wafted to the island of Cythera, just west of Crete. For this reason, she is called both Cytherean Aphrodite and Cypriote Aphrodite. When Aphrodite floated ashore, a group of nymphs clothed her and became her loyal attendants.

Arriving at Mount Olympus

After some time, the nymphs took beautiful Aphrodite to Mount Olympus, home of the gods. The gods welcomed her as one of their own and gave her a golden throne to sit on. Because she was so beautiful, many of the gods fell in love with her and wanted to marry her.

Zeus did not want the gods to fight over Aphrodite. He decided that he would choose a husband for her. He chose sturdy and gentle Hephaestus, the god of fire and the patron god of blacksmiths. Aphrodite was not happy with the marriage, for Hephaestus was the ugliest of the Olympian gods. Also,

Aphrodite, goddess of love, is represented in this marble statue. The statue is a Roman copy of a Greek original of the fifth century B.C. It can be viewed at the Galleria Borghese in Rome, Italy.

he was always filthy with dust from working in his hot forge.

Hephaestus wanted to please Aphrodite nonetheless. He did everything he could to make her happy, producing the most beautiful gifts in order to please her. He forged stunning pieces of jewelry with precious metals and sparkling gems. He even made her clothes woven from threads of pure gold. Hephaestus fashioned a magic belt for her, which made her even more beautiful. In the end, however, his gifts were not enough to satisfy Aphrodite.

In Love with War

Aphrodite did not want to be the wife of Hephaestus—he was ugly, he spent most of his time working in his forge, and he was too gentle and reserved for her. She soon fell in love with Hephaestus's brother, Ares, the god of war.

Aphrodite was drawn to Ares because of his handsome face and confident ways, and she agreed to steal away with him for romantic meetings. Aphrodite's affection for Ares did not remain a secret for

CLXXIV

Aphrodite (continued)

long. When Helios, the god of the Sun, told Hephaestus that his wife had fallen in love with his arrogant brother, Hephaestus was furious.

In his anger, Hephaestus decided to take revenge on them both. He fashioned an invisible net and carefully placed it over Aphrodite's bed. When Ares and Aphrodite returned, Hephaestus caught them in the net and called the other gods to come and see. They all laughed when they saw Ares and Aphrodite caught together.

Aphrodite paid little attention to Hephaestus and they never had any children together. Even though Hephaestus had proven his cunning in catching his wife and Ares together, he could not stop Aphrodite's love for Ares.

Aphrodite and Ares had three children together. Their daughter, Harmonia, eventually married Cadmus, the founder of Thebes. Their two sons, Deimos, the spirit of Panic, and Phobos, the spirit of Fear, soon became regular companions of Ares as he rode his chariot into battle. With his sons riding with him, the sight of Ares was more terrifying than ever before.

Aphrodite was also the mother of Eros and his brother, Anteros. Eros flew all over the world on golden wings, shooting mortals with arrows guaranteed to hit their target. When people were struck with the arrow of Eros, they would fall in love with the first person they saw. Anteros was the god of mutual love and he punished mortals who did not return the love of others.

Aphrodite loved Ares, but she had many mortal lovers as well. One was Adonis, one of the most beautiful young men ever to live. When Adonis was killed by a wild boar, Aphrodite was heartbroken. Aphrodite also fell in love with the mortal, Anchises. They became the parents of Aeneas, the great Trojan hero.

Who Is the Fairest Goddess?

Aphrodite played a vital role in the Trojan War. She was the mother of the brave Trojan warrior Aeneas. Aphrodite was also directly involved in the abduction of Helen.

Long before the Trojan War, all the gods were invited to a wedding on Mount Olympus. The only god not invited was Eris, the goddess of strife, because she was a notorious troublemaker. Eris was furious at the slight. She stormed up to Mount Olympus to disrupt the ceremony.

During the celebration, Eris threw a golden apple, the apple of discord, among the guests. The apple bore the inscription "To the fairest." Hera, Athena, and Aphrodite all rushed for the apple, each one believing it was meant for her. An intense argument between the three goddesses ensued, ruining the wedding. Zeus was forced to intervene.

Zeus appointed Paris, a handsome prince from Troy, to decide which of the three goddesses would receive the apple. Each goddess offered him a gift in exchange for the apple: Hera offered him political power; Athena promised him wisdom; and Aphrodite proposed he would have the most beautiful woman in the world as his wife. Without much hesitation, Paris awarded the apple to Aphrodite.

At that time, the most beautiful woman in the world was Helen, the wife of King Menelaus of Sparta. Aphrodite sent Eros to shoot Helen with his love-arrows, and Paris sailed to Sparta soon after. Helen was enchanted by handsome Paris and the two ran off together.

Angered by the loss of his wife, Menelaus and his brother, Agamemnon, assembled an enormous Greek army to sail to Troy to recover Helen. This was the start of the Trojan War.

Taking the Side of the Trojans

During the course of the Trojan War, Aphrodite and Ares fought

Aphrodite was the goddess of love. She was associated with roses, swans, and doves.

alongside the Trojans. Aphrodite was not a skilled warrior. She was wounded by the Greek hero Diomedes when she tried to defend her son, Aeneas. She then fled to Olympus, where her wounds were healed.

Because Aphrodite spent much of her time with Ares, many ancient Greeks believed that she was also a war goddess. Some ancient artists depicted her carrying a spear and shield. Other artists showed Aphrodite carrying Nike, the winged spirit of victory.

Many ancient Greeks called their love-goddess *Aphrodite Urania*, which means Heavenly Aphrodite. This was because Aphrodite was also related to storms, lightning, and weather in general and Urania was the Muse of astronomy. Aphrodite's relationship to weather may explain why many of her grandest temples were built at the tops of hills or mountains, where the changing weather could be observed easily.

Like the other Olympian gods, Aphrodite was quick to punish any mortal who failed to offer proper sacrifices to her. Aphrodite was generally a happy, smiling goddess who rewarded her most devout followers.

See also Venus; Eros; Cupid; Ares; Mars; Hephaestus; Vulcan; Adonis; Anchises; Aeneas; Paris; Muses; Pygmalion.

FAMILY: Husband was Hephaestus; sons were Eros, Anteros, Deimos, Phobos, and Hymen; daughter was Harmonia.

IN ART: One of the earliest Greek sculptures to expose the human body was an artistic representation of Aphrodite. The sculpture is called the *Aphrodite of Knidos*. It was produced around 350 B.C. by the Athenian sculptor Praxiteles. The *Aphrodite of Knidos* became one of the most celebrated pieces of art in the ancient world. In book 36 of *Natural History*, the Roman writer Pliny the Elder told of the spectacular setting where ancient

Aphrodite (continued)

people viewed the *Aphrodite of Knidos.* Pliny described the statue standing in the middle of a circular temple dedicated to Aphrodite, where it could be viewed from all sides. (Later, when Aphrodite became known as Venus to the Romans, copies of *Aphrodite of Knidos* were produced. The *Venus of Arles* is an example of a Roman copy of Praxiteles's work.)

Sometimes artworks were known by both the Greek and Roman names for the goddess. An example is one of the most famous sculptures in the world, best known as the *Venus de Milo,* associating it with Aphrodite's Roman counterpart. This sculpture was known as the *Aphrodite of Melos* when it was created in 150 B.C. The sculptor, Alexandros, worked near the city of Antioch, which lies in modern-day Syria. The statue takes its name from the Greek island of Melos, where it was discovered in 1820. The *Venus de Milo* is on display in the Louvre Museum in Paris, France.

Another famous sculpture of Aphrodite shows her and her son Eros fighting off the advances of Pan, a satyr (half man, half goat). The satyrs were known for chasing beautiful women. In the sculpture, Aphrodite appears ready to strike Pan with her sandal, while Eros holds him by the horn. This statue

was created around 100 B.C. on the island of Delos. The inscription on the base of the statue reads: *Dionysios, son of Zeno, son of Theodoros of Berytus, benefactor, [dedicates this] on behalf of himself and of his children to the ancestral gods.*

Aphrodite's Roman counterpart, Venus, was the subject of paintings by several European artists. *See* Venus.

IN LITERATURE: In the *Theogony* (literally, "Birth of the Gods"), Hesiod gives an account of how Aphrodite was born. He also explains the origins of the different names of Aphrodite:

> …and a white foam spread around them from the immortal flesh, and in it there grew a maiden.
>
> First she drew near holy Cythera, and from there, afterwards, she came to sea-girt Cyprus, and came forth an awful and lovely goddess, and grass grew up about her beneath her shapely feet.
>
> Her gods and men call Aphrodite, and the foam-born goddess and rich-crowned Cythera, because she grew amid the foam, and Cythera because she reached Cythera
>
> *Hesiod, Theogony, lines 191–198; translation by Hugh G. Evelyn-White*

Throughout the literature of ancient Greece, Aphrodite often opposes three Olympian goddesses—Athena, Artemis, and Hestia—because they are chaste

and never marry. In some written works, Aphrodite is angry that she has no power over them. This tension is described in this passage from *Homeric Hymn 5 to Aphrodite:*

> Yet there are three hearts that she cannot bend nor yet ensnare.
>
> First is the daughter of Zeus who holds the aegis, bright-eyed Athene; for she has no pleasure in the deeds of golden Aphrodite, but delights in wars and in the work of Ares, in strifes and battles and in preparing famous crafts…
>
> Nor does laughter-loving Aphrodite ever tame in love Artemis, the huntress with shafts of gold; for she loves archery and the slaying of wild beasts in the mountains…
>
> Nor yet does the pure maiden Hestia love Aphrodite's works… a queenly maid whom both Poseidon and Apollo sought to wed.
>
> But she was wholly unwilling, nay, stubbornly refused; and touching the head of father Zeus who holds the aegis, she, that fair goddess, sware a great oath which has in truth been fulfilled, that she would be a maiden all her days.
>
> *Homeric Hymn 5 to Aphrodite, lines 7–11, 16–18, 21–22, 24–28; translation by Hugh G. Evelyn-White*

There are also numerous mentions of Aphrodite throughout modern literature, including works by William Shakespeare, Lord Byron, John Keats, and John Milton.

"...and a white foam spread around them from the immortal flesh, and in it there grew a maiden."

—Hesiod's *Theogony*

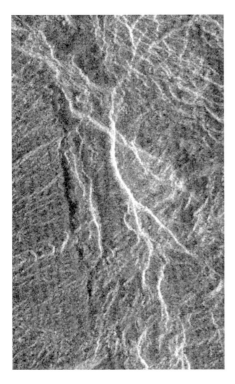

NASA's Magellan spacecraft captured this image of Aphrodite Terra, a mountainous region on the planet Venus. Aphrodite Terra, a region about the size of the continent of Africa, lies near Venus's equator.

IN SPACE: The second-closest planet to the Sun in the solar system is Venus, named for Aphrodite's Roman counterpart. On Venus, there is a mountainous region called the *Aphrodite Terra*. This large region is roughly the same size as the continent of Africa. Aphrodite Terra lies close to the planet's equator.

IN SCIENCE: The name Aphrodite has been used frequently to name plants and animals. The goddess lends her name to the family of sea worms *Aphroditidae,* the genera *Aphrodite,* and the species *aphrodite.* Many of the plants and animals named for Aphrodite are marine organisms, which relates to Aphrodite's birth from the sea.

A butterfly, *Speyeria aphrodite,* is commonly known as the Aphrodite Fritillary butterfly.

WORD HISTORY: The name Aphrodite is derived from the Greek word *aphros,* which means "foam". It is a reference to the birth of Aphrodite from the foam of the sea. An *aphrodisiac* is a love potion meant to stimulate love or desire. An *hermaphrodite* is an animal or plant that has both male and female reproductive organs. Its name comes from Hemaphroditus, a son of Hermes and Aphrodite whose body joined with the body of a nymph.

MODERN USAGE: The tradition of sending roses to someone you love may stem from the story of Aphrodite. Roses were a favorite flower to this goddess of love.

The myrtle tree was also sacred to Aphrodite. In Myrtle Beach, South Carolina, a tradition began of holding beauty contests for women in bathing suits. Beautiful women would pose in front of Aphrodite's myrtle trees and have their pictures taken.

GO TO THE SOURCE: The stories of Aphrodite are scattered throughout ancient Greek literature. There are three *Homeric Hymns to Aphrodite.* (There are 34 *Homeric Hymns* that most experts believe were written several centuries after Homer lived.) The goddess appears in Homer's *Iliad* and *Odyssey* as well. The story of Ares, Aphrodite, and Hephaestus is told in book 8 of Homer's *Odyssey.* Hesiod also mentions Aphrodite in his works, especially in the *Theogony.* An account of Uranian (Heavenly) Aphrodite can be found in Plato's *Symposium.* Information on the goddess can be found in the *Library* and *Epitome* by Apollodorus. Pausanias's *Description of Greece* and Herodotus's *History* (especially books 1 and 2) contain numerous references to how the ancient Greeks worshiped Aphrodite. Greek playwrights, including Aeschylus, Sophocles, and Aristophanes, mention Aphrodite in their works. Aphrodite has a major role in the *Hippolytus* by Euripides. The Greek goddess of love was also a common subject in the works of Sappho, a female Greek poet who lived in the seventh century B.C.

Apollo

Απολλων

PRONUNCIATION: uh-PAWL-oh

EQUIVALENT CHARACTER: Apollo was also known as Phoebus, meaning "bright one."

GENDER: Male

CULTURE: Greek and Roman

ATTRIBUTES: Light; Reason; Music; Poetry; Prophecy; the Sun; Art; Medicine; Beauty

To the Greeks, golden-haired Apollo represented physical perfection. Apollo was the god of light, music, poetry, and reason. He was the commander of the Muses and made beautiful music on the lyre. The laurel, whose leaves are used to crown the heads of poets, was sacred to him. Apollo and his twin sister, Artemis, were the children of Zeus, the king of the Olympian gods.

Zeus looked down on the Earth one day and fell in love with Leto, a beautiful young woman. He decided to be with her. Zeus knew that his wife, Hera, would be jealous, so he transformed himself into a swan so Hera would not see them together.

Soon Leto became pregnant. Zeus had many love affairs, but he was never able to keep his loves secret from Hera for long. Eventually Hera found out about Leto. She became angrier when she learned that Leto and Zeus were going to have a baby together. She declared that Leto would not be able to give birth in any place the Sun shone.

Leto was distraught, and wandered all over Greece looking for a place to give birth. No one welcomed her, for they feared Hera's wrath. Leto finally arrived at Delos, an island so new that it floated on top of the sea. The people who lived there welcomed her. In the shade of a palm tree Leto gave birth to the divine twin children of

Apollo was the god of music, light, shepherds, and medicine. His twin sister was Artemis, the goddess of the hunt. Apollo was thought to be young and beautiful, and an excellent athlete. He also had the power to see the future. People would come to Apollo's temple at Delphi to ask his advice about the future.

Zeus. First to be born was Artemis, a beautiful girl with hair as black as night. Within minutes of her birth, Artemis helped her mother give birth to Apollo, whose golden hair and skin shone like the Sun.

Before long Zeus took Apollo and Artemis to Mount Olympus to live among the gods. Artemis

TRUE OR FALSE?

1. Apollo was the son of Zeus and Leto.
2. Apollo and Artemis were twins.
3. Apollo was the god of the hunt and wild animals.
4. Apollo was in love with Eros.
5. Apollo was associated with the oracle of Delphi.
6. The laurel tree was sacred to Apollo.
7. Apollo got his lyre from the Satyr Marsyas.
8. The Muses were followers of Apollo.

Apollo (continued)

became the goddess of the hunt and of all wild animals. Apollo became the god of light, music, poetry, and reason. Zeus gave silver bows and arrows to Artemis and Apollo. They became known as the gods of archery and were worshiped throughout the ancient world.

Apollo Learns to Predict the Future

When he was just four days old, Apollo learned to predict the future. He learned this from Pan, the goat-legged god of shepherds and forests. Apollo then went to Delphi, the most sacred place in all of Greece. Living there was a priestess who, like Apollo, also practiced divination (predicting the future).

The area around Delphi was guarded by Python, a horrible serpent. When Apollo approached, Python lunged at him, spitting fire and poison. But Apollo was not afraid. Even though he was only four days old, Apollo reached for his bow and began shooting his silver arrows. He did not stop shooting at Python until its huge body crashed to the ground, lifeless, with a thousand silver arrows buried in its side.

Apollo claimed Delphi for his own. Apollo's head priestess at Delphi became known as the

Pythia in honor of Apollo's conquest of Python.

Soon Apollo was one of the most important of the Olympian gods. Kings and commoners alike traveled from all over the ancient world to consult the oracle at Delphi.

Greeks and Romans raised temples to Apollo and celebrated him as a god of light and reason. Ancient people also worshiped Apollo's sister Artemis and his mother Leto. The three lived con-

Apollo, the god of light and music, is often shown wearing a laurel wreath, because of its association with Daphne, his beloved, who was turned into a laurel tree.

tentedly with the other gods on Mount Olympus.

It Is Dangerous to Insult the Gods

One day Niobe, the arrogant mortal queen of Thebes, declared to the Theban people that she was as beautiful as Leto. Niobe also proclaimed herself superior to Leto because she had seven beautiful daughters and seven handsome sons, while Leto had only one daughter and one son.

Artemis and Apollo were furious. Mortals could not compare themselves to the gods without expecting severe consequences. The twin gods descended to Earth to take revenge on Niobe. Artemis shot Niobe's daughters with her silver arrows, killing them instantly. Apollo used his arrows to kill Niobe's seven sons. With all her children dead, the grief-stricken Niobe now knew it was a mistake to offend the gods. Niobe wept for countless days and weeks. At last Zeus took pity on her and turned her to stone. Niobe's sorrow was so great that the rock continued to weep for all eternity.

A Love-Arrow Strikes

Apollo was proud of the power of his bow and arrow. He didn't want any other god to claim the right to use the same weapon. Another god who liked the bow and arrow was Eros, the god of love. Apollo told Eros to put away his bow and arrow. Apollo said the bow and arrow was his weapon exclusively.

Eros was outraged. Eros's arrows were love-arrows. Eros used them to inspire romance. Eros decided to teach Apollo a lesson about the power of his love-arrows. He drew back his bow and shot Apollo through the heart with one. After the love-arrow struck, Apollo's gaze fell on the beautiful Daphne—and he fell hopelessly in love with her.

Eros did not choose a love-arrow for Daphne, however. Instead, he drew a lead-tipped arrow from his quiver, which had the opposite effect. When this arrow pierced Daphne's heart, the first person she saw was Apollo. She turned and ran away. Apollo pursued her and quickly overtook her. The frightened Daphne called out for help to her father, the river god Peneus.

At the first touch of Apollo's hand, Daphne's skin grew rough and hard, and her legs became rooted to the ground. Peneus had

This detail of a frieze (a decorative band of artwork) depicts (from left to right) Aphrodite with her son, Eros; Apollo, god of music, with his lyre; Athena, goddess of wisdom and warfare, wearing her warrior's helmet; and three of the Muses. The frieze is on the walls of the museum at the Chateaux de Malmaison et Bois-Preau, the former residence of Napoleon Bonaparte, near Paris, France.

Apollo (continued)

changed his daughter into a laurel tree! Apollo's love was true, and he vowed to make the laurel his sacred tree.

Apollo Gets the *Lyre* and the *Syrinx*

Apollo had many talents, but his greatest gift was music. The story of how Apollo got his instrument, the *lyre,* involves a baby, some cows, and a tortoise.

Hermes, the messenger of the gods, was born a hungry and very clever baby. On the day he was born, Hermes slipped away from his sleeping mother and ventured toward the field where Apollo kept his herd of cows. He chose the fifty best cows and stole them, leading them by their tails so that their tracks would point toward their own field. He herded the cows away and sacrificed two of them to the gods. Hermes then made a meal of some of the cows. With his hunger satisfied, he hurried back to his home.

Just then a giant tortoise crawled by. Hermes killed the tortoise and hollowed out its shell. Then he stretched some of the cows' intestines across the opening of the shell to make strings. When he was finished he had created the first *lyre.*

By now Apollo discovered that his prize cows were missing. He was anxious to find them, but was confused by their tracks, which led only to an empty field. This was a mystery! Apollo went to Delphi to consult the oracle. He could hardly believe his ears when the oracle revealed that baby Hermes was the thief.

Apollo stormed off to find Hermes asleep in his cradle. He snatched up the baby, woke him and accused him of stealing his sacred cows. Hermes pretended to know nothing. Hermes' mother scolded Apollo for accusing her one-day-old baby of the theft, but Apollo knew that the oracle had told him the truth. Apollo carried Hermes to Mount Olympus, where he could make the accusation in front of Zeus.

Hermes again tried to deny the robbery, but Zeus had seen everything. He forced Hermes to return the cattle to Apollo.

To charm the gods Hermes brought forth his creation, the lyre, and began plucking the strings. The music overpowered Apollo, and he offered to trade his cows for the lyre. Baby Hermes agreed and went back to Earth to tend his herd of prize cows.

During the hours spent watching the cows, the clever Hermes invented another instrument—the *syrinx.* When Apollo heard the sweet melodies Hermes played on the syrinx, a shepherd's pipe, he begged Hermes for the instrument. This time Apollo offered to trade a golden shepherd's staff. Hermes accepted. From that day on, Apollo was rarely seen without his lyre and syrinx. The gods on Mount Olympus were delighted when he played for them. Mortals on Earth, inspired by Apollo's music, began playing the lyre and the syrinx themselves.

Apollo Is Challenged

Inspired by Apollo, the love of music spread throughout the ancient world. Many mortals became master musicians, but none dared to compare himself to Apollo, one of the mighty gods of Mount Olympus. The satyr, Marsyas, was the only one to ever challenge Apollo in a musical contest. Apollo accepted the satyr's challenge, but warned him that he would lose his skin if he lost the contest. The two contestants then agreed that each would nominate judges to make a decision on their competition.

Marsyas appointed King Midas to be a judge; Apollo appointed his loyal followers, the Muses. (The nine Muses were Calliope, the Muse of Epic Poetry; Clio, the Muse of History; Erato, the Muse of Lyric Poetry; Euterpe, the Muse of Music; Melpomene, the Muse of Tragedy; Thalia, the Muse of

Inside the Temple of Apollo at Delphi, situated on Mount Parnassus, sat Pythia, the priestess who was said to receive prophecies from Apollo. Pan taught Apollo to predict the future when he was just four days old.

Comedy; Terpsichore, the Muse of Dance; Polyhymnia, the Muse of Hymns; Urania, the Muse of Astronomy.)

Apollo performed first, playing a magnificent song praising the gods on his lyre. It was then the satyr's turn, and he played a cheerful melody on his double flute. The Muses cast their one vote for Apollo, but Midas named Marsyas the winner. Apollo then turned his lyre upside-down and played even better than before. He ordered Marsyas to do the same, but no sound came out when the satyr blew through his upside-down flute.

Apollo was declared the winner and made good on his warning, skinning Marsyas alive. All of a sudden, King Midas's head began to sprout donkey ears! Apollo caused this to happen so that Midas would not go unpunished for choosing Marsyas as the better musician.

Again and again, Apollo showed himself to be a vengeful god when mortal men angered him. During the Trojan War, the Greek leader Agamemnon captured the daughter of Chryses, one of Apollo's priests. Chryses prayed to Apollo to punish the Greeks, and Apollo answered the prayer. For nine days Apollo brought a plague on the Greek army, and many soldiers died. On the tenth day, Agamemnon released Chryses's daughter, and Apollo stopped the plague.

See also Artemis; Diana; Niobe; Daphne; Hermes; Marsyas; Midas; Muses; Helios; Sol.

FAMILY: Father was Zeus (Roman Jupiter); mother was Leto (Roman Latona); twin sister was Artemis (Roman Diana); son was Asclepius.

IN ART: In ancient times, Apollo was represented in art more frequently than any other god. Portraits of him usually combine manhood with everlasting youth.

Apollo (continued)

A statue of Apollo once stood on the west pediment of the Temple of Zeus at Olympia. The statue, completed around 460 B.C., depicts Apollo as the ideal youth, both strong and handsome, as his outstretched arm brings peace. It now stands in the Olympia Museum in Athens, Greece.

Many ancient vase paintings feature depictions of Apollo, including one where Apollo and Artemis are killing the children of vain Niobe with their bows and arrows. This vase was completed around 465 B.C. and may be seen in the Louvre Museum in Paris, France.

The *Apollo Belvedere,* a sculpture completed around 320 B.C. by Leochares of Athens, was regarded by the ancient Greeks as one of the greatest examples of the beauty of the human form. The *Apollo Belvedere* that survives to the modern day is not the original, but a Roman copy of the Greek statue. This copy may be viewed in the Pio Clementino Museum in Vatican City in Italy.

Many artists have been inspired by the story of Apollo and Daphne. One example is *Apollo and Daphne,* a sculpture in white marble completed around 1625 by the Italian artist Giovanni Lorenzo Bernini. This piece depicts the moment when Daphne calls to her father for help and he transforms her into a laurel tree. The trunk of the tree has just begun to form around her legs, and her fingers have just started sprouting leaves. This sculpture is displayed in the Borghese Museum and Gallery in Rome, Italy.

IN LITERATURE: In the epic poem, the *Iliad,* Homer described the scene during the Trojan War when Chryses, a priest of Apollo, prayed to his patron god for revenge against Agamemnon. Apollo answered his prayer and sent suffering to the Greeks for nine days. In this passage, Homer described Apollo's actions:

> In answer to the prayer, Phoebus Apollo, enraged in his heart, came down from the heights of Olympus, carrying his bow and quivers on his shoulder. And the arrows clattered as he stomped in his rage. He came like night, and he shot his silver bow with a dreadful twang. At first, he struck the mules and dogs in the camp. But then he aimed his pointed shafts at the men themselves, and he hit them. And the funeral pyres for all the dead were burning fast and furious.
>
> *Homer,* Iliad, *book 1, lines 43–52; translation by Rick M. Newton*

The Romans also wrote about Apollo. In his poem, the *Metamorphoses,* Ovid described how Apollo mourned for his love, Daphne, after she was transformed into a laurel tree:

> A down-dragging numbness seized her limbs, and her soft sides were begirt with thin bark.
>
> Her hair was changed to leaves, her arms to branches.
>
> Her feet, but now so swift, grew fast in sluggish roots, and her head was now but a tree's top.
>
> Her gleaming beauty alone remained.
>
> But even now in this new form Apollo loved her...and the god cried out to this:
>
> "Since thou canst be my bride, thou shalt at least be my tree. My hair, my lyre, my quiver shall always be entwined with thee, O laurel. With thee shall Roman generals wreathe their heads, when shouts of joy shall acclaim their triumph"
>
> *Ovid,* Metamorphoses, *book 1, lines 549–553, 557–562; translation by Frank Justus Miller*

Much later, the Elizabethan poet William Shakespeare referred to Apollo as the god and patron of music and learning. In *Love's Labour's Lost* he used a simile:

> As sweet and musical as bright Apollo's lute, strung with his hair.

In *A Winter's Tale* Shakespeare invokes Apollo for his gift of clairvoyance, when the character Leontes consults the oracle at Delphi.

The nineteenth-century English poet John Keats composed a

poem, *Hymn to Apollo.* This passage is from the first stanza:

> God of the golden bow,
> And of the golden lyre,
> And of the golden hair,
> And of the golden fire,
> Charioteer
> Of the patient year,
> Where—where slept thine ire,
> When like a blank idiot I put on thy
>   wreath,
> Thy laurel, thy glory,
> The light of thy story,
> Or was I a worm—too low crawling
>   for death?
> O Delphic Apollo!

The *Hymn of Apollo* written by the English poet Percy Bysshe Shelley includes stanzas that are speeches made by Apollo himself:

> Then I arise, and climbing heaven's
>   blue dome
> I walk over the mountains and the
>   waves,
> Leaving my robe upon the ocean
>   foam

IN SPACE: In 1932, German astronomer Karl Reinmuth discovered the Apollo asteroids, some of which have orbits that cross over the Earth's orbit. In 1961, U.S. president John F. Kennedy announced the Apollo Space Program, which was aimed at landing an astronaut on the Moon. On July 20, 1969, the world watched the culmination of this program as three astronauts (Neil Armstrong,

In 1969, the Apollo 11 mission sent astronauts to the Moon. This photo, taken by Neil Armstrong, shows "Buzz" Aldrin setting up instruments on the Moon's surface. The Lunar Module Eagle is in the background.

Edwin "Buzz" Aldrin, and Michael Collins) landed on the Moon.

WORD HISTORY: *Apollonian* is an adjective used to describe a person with the characteristics of the Greek god Apollo (such as physical beauty).

As a philosophical term, *Apollonian* describes the human

Corvus: The Crow

In ancient Greece and Rome it was believed that this constellation represented a crow, the messenger-bird of Apollo.

An ancient myth tells of how the crow got black feathers. Apollo, the god of light and music, was once married to beautiful Coronis.

Apollo's favorite bird was the crow, which at that time had white feathers. One day, the crow came to Apollo and told him that he had seen Coronis with another man. Apollo became so angry that he shot Coronis through the heart with one of his piercing arrows.

Afterwards, Apollo was grief-stricken at the loss of his love. As an expression of his grief, Apollo turned the crow's feathers black.

The brightest star in Corvus is (1) Gienah corvi, which means "the crow's wing." This is a blue giant star, but astronomers predict that it will become a red giant in millions of years. Gienah corvi is close to 165 light-years from Earth, and is about 355 times brighter than the Sun.

Till Credner/allthesky.com

love for balance, order, and symmetry. German philosopher Frederich Nietzsche maintans that all human beings have an Apollonian desire for reason and neatness. *See also* Bacchus.

A *paean* is a hymn of praise or thanksgiving; in ancient Greece, paean was a word associated with Apollo and songs of thanksgiving dedicated to him.

MODERN USAGE: The landmark Apollo Theater in New York City was named for the god of music. Many musicians—including Ella Fitzgerald, Michael Jackson, and Lauryn Hill—have appeared at the Apollo.

The tradition of placing a laurel wreath on the head of the victor in an athletic competition was inspired by Apollo, who considered the laurel sacred. The tradition was carried forward at the 2004 Summer Olympic Games in Athens, Greece. Every gold-medal winner at those Olympics wore a laurel wreath on the victory stand.

GO TO THE SOURCE: Nearly every ancient Greek and Roman author wrote about Apollo. Hesiod included references to Apollo in his poem, the *Theogony*. Homer wrote about Apollo in both the *Iliad* and the *Odyssey*. The *Homeric Hymn to Apollo* described the worship of the god, but was probably not written by Homer. (There are 34 *Homeric Hymns* that most experts believe were written several centuries after Homer lived.)

Other Greek authors also wrote about Apollo. Apollodorus wrote about the god in his two works, the *Library* and the *Epitome*. Pausanias's work, *Description of Greece,* and Hyginus's work, the *Fables,* both included references to Apollo. Apollo plays a major role in the *Eumenides* by Aeschylus, but he is only mentioned in other Greek tragedies. Apollo's sacred oracle at Delphi is consulted throughout the *History* by Herodotus.

Numerous Roman authors also wrote of Apollo. The stories of Apollo and his relationships with Daphne and Niobe are found in the *Metamorphoses* by Ovid. Livy's *History of Rome* provided valuable information about the worship of Apollo by the people of ancient Rome.

Apollodorus

Απολλοδωρος

Apollodorus was a Greek scholar who may have lived during the second century B.C. Recent scholars suggest that he lived in the first or second century A.D. He was believed to be a student of the scholar Aristarchus and the philosopher Panaetius.

Apollodorus is believed to have written a large number of books, but only fragments from a few of them have been preserved throughout the centuries. Most of his books were on the subjects of history, mythology, grammar, and geography.

His book *Chronica* was written in poetic verse and relates important details of Greek history after the fall of Troy. His *On the Gods* was a multivolume work on mythology. Another book on mythology called *Bibliotheca,* or *The Library,* was published under the name of Apollodorus, but scholars debate whether he was the real author of the work.

Appian

Appian (c.95–c.165) was a Greek historian who lived in Alexandria, Egypt. There is very little information known about his early life. However, there is evidence that he held some type of public office in Alexandria before going to Rome to practice law. There he met Emperor Antoninus Pius, who appointed Appian to the position of imperial procurator in Egypt. In this position, Appian was an overseer of civil affairs, finances, tax collection, and estate management on behalf of the emperor.

Throughout his public career, Appian was a careful student of history. As a historian, he wrote several books, but only a small number of them were preserved in their complete form. Fragments of other works have been discovered and preserved as well.

His most famous collection, usually called the *Roman History,* was a 24 volume set that covered a time period from the early development of the Roman Empire to the reign of Emperor Trajan (98–117). Only 11 volumes of this collection were preserved in their complete form. The most well-known of these was *Civil Wars,* which serves as the earliest account on this topic ever discovered. *Foreign Wars* has also been an important resource for students of early Roman history.

Arachne

Αραχνη

PRONUNCIATION: uh-RAK-nee
GENDER: Female
CULTURE: Roman
ATTRIBUTES: Weaving; Pride

Arachne was a princess who lived in Lydia, a region in Asia Minor. She challenged the goddess Minerva to a weaving contest, which Minerva won.

Arachne was a princess in the kingdom of Lydia in Asia Minor. Arachne was a skillful weaver and her reputation extended far beyond her home. Admirers came from far away to watch her at her loom. Even the forest nymphs left their woodland home to admire Arachne's handiwork. Arachne became so proud and confident of her weaving skills that she challenged the goddess Minerva, the patron of all handicrafts, to a weaving contest.

The gods never looked kindly on mortals who challenged them, and Minerva was no exception. Although Arachne's challenge angered and offended her, Minerva agreed to the competition. Arachne and Minerva took their places at their looms and began to weave.

Crowds gathered to watch as the two worked quickly, each using threads of every color. Minerva wove a beautiful scene depicting the Olympian gods sitting on their thrones. Those watching agreed that Minerva had created a perfect tapestry. Arachne then revealed her tapestry, which also depicted the gods, but in scenes less glorious than Minerva's. Everyone agreed that Arachne's weaving was as fine as Minerva's.

Minerva was angry. She wanted to win the contest, and she felt Arachne's work was disrespectful of the gods. In a rage Minerva shredded Arachne's weaving. Arachne was so humiliated that she hanged herself. Just when life was about to escape Arachne's body, Minerva took pity on her and loosened the noose around Arachne's neck. But that was the end of Minerva's mercy. She let Arachne live, but she changed the noose into a spider's web and transformed Arachne into a spider.

From that day on, Arachne's weaving skill produced only intricate spider webs. Minerva made sure Arachne would never again insult the gods. Whenever the ancients would see a spider hanging on its own thread, they thought of poor Arachne hanging in her own web.

FAMILY: Father was Idmon.

IN ART: A frieze decorating the ancient walls of the colonnade of the Forum Nervae in Rome, Italy, shows the punishment of Arachne by Minerva. (A frieze is a horizontal band of decoration.) The seventeenth-century Spanish artist Diego Velazquez composed *Las Hilanderas* (*The Spinners* or *The Fable of Arachne*), a large painting that depicts the story of Arachne. It hangs in the Prado Museum in Madrid, Spain.

TRUE OR FALSE?

1. Arachne was a skilled weaver.
2. Arachne challenged Minerva to a cooking contest.
3. Minerva changed Arachne into a butterfly.
4. Arachnids get their name from Arachne.
5. Arachnophobia is the fear of webs.

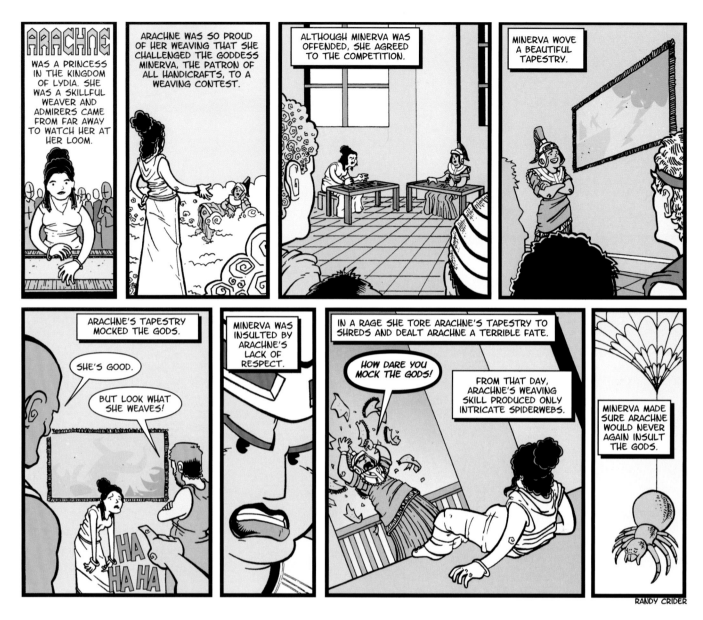

RANDY CRIDER

IN LITERATURE: The English Renaissance poet Edmund Spenser wrote about Arachne in his poem *Muiopotmos,* also known as *The Fate of the Butterflie.* He refers to Pallas (for Pallas Athena), one of the Greek names for Minerva:

> The most fine-fingred workwoman
>   on ground,
> Arachne, by his meanes was
>   vanquished
> Of Pallas, and in her owne skill
>   confound,
> When she with her for excellence
>   contended,
> That wrought her shame, and
>   sorrow neuer ended.

> For the Tritonian goddesse, hauing
>   hard
> Her blazed fame, which all the
>   world had fil'd,
> Came downe to proue the truth,
>   and due reward
> For her prais-worthie workmanship
>   to yeild
> But the presumptuous Damzel
>   rashly dar'd
> The Goddesse selfe to chalenge to
>   the field,
> And to compare with her in curious
>   skill
> Of workes with loome, with needle,
>   and with quill.

William Shakespeare alluded to Arachne when, in his play, *Troilus and Cressida* he speaks of "Arachne's broken woof'," meaning a thread of cobweb.

WORD HISTORY: Spiders or *arachnids* get their name from Arachne. *Arachnophobia* is the fear of spiders.

GO TO THE SOURCE: The only ancient author to write of Arachne was the Roman poet Ovid. The famous contest between Arachne and Minerva can be found at the beginning of book 6 of Ovid's *Metamorphoses.*

Ares

Αρης

PRONUNCIATION: AIR-eez

EQUIVALENT CHARACTER: The Roman god Mars

GENDER: Male

CULTURE: Greek

ATTRIBUTES: War; Arrogance; Rashness; Handsome but dull-witted

Ares was the Greek god of war. He was the most cruel and arrogant of all the Olympian gods. When he rode into battle on his chariot, Ares always struck fear into mortal men.

As the god of war and battles, Ares was a symbol of raw power, delighting in bloodshed and war for its own sake. He was hated by all the Olympian gods except Aphrodite, who loved him. His emblems were the spear and the burning torch, symbolizing the devastation of war. He had flaming red hair. In fact, throwing a lit torch was the signal for the start of a battle in ancient Greece. The sacred animals of Ares were the dog and the vulture.

A God Who Loved to Fight

Ares was the son of Zeus and Hera, the king and queen of all the Olympian gods. More than anything, Ares enjoyed entering the field of battle, either in his chariot or on foot. Ares preferred to fight wildly, relying on brute strength and blind rage to steer him toward victory.

Ares as a "god of war" differed significantly from Athena, his half sister and another god of war. While Athena presided over the strategic intelligence that is always useful and often necessary to win a difficult battle, the god Ares presided over the madness and furor of raging war that drives soldiers to commit atrocities and uncontrolled acts of nonsensical violence.

Because they were so different, Athena and Ares hated one another and fought on opposite

Ares loved to fight so much that he would join in mortal battles, brutally killing whoever stood in his way. All men were terrified when they saw Ares on the battlefield.

sides in the Trojan War. Athena, as the protector of Greek cities, fought alongside the Greeks, while Ares and his lover Aphrodite, the goddess of love, sided with the Trojans. *See* Athena.

When Ares arrived on the battlefield, men would become terrified. Ares did not care which side won or lost—he just wanted to fight. As long as blood was being shed, Ares was probably having a good time.

TRUE OR FALSE?

1. Ares was the Greek god of war.
2. The horse was a sacred animal to Ares.
3. Ares loved his half-sister Athena.
4. Various war spirits followed Ares into battle.
5. Ares and Aphrodite were enemies.
6. Ares was the father of Eros, the god of love.
7. In most artwork, Ares wears a plumed helmet and carries a shield and spear.

Ares (continued)

Ares would charge into the middle of battles between mortal men, hacking and cutting whoever stood in his way. Ares was always accompanied by various war spirits who would make mortal men even more terrified.

One war spirit was Ares' sister, Eris, the goddess of discord and strife. She turned friends against one another and forced enemies to go to war. Enyo, another spirit who allied herself with Ares, was a war goddess who especially took pleasure in sacking cities. Ares' two sons, Deimos and Phobos (Panic and Fear), were also his regular companions, and it was their responsibility to prepare his war chariot. Finally, the Keres, goddesses of death, followed Ares into battle. Their job was to search for dead bodies to bring to the realm of Hades.

Romance Strikes Ares

Many feared Ares and avoided him, but Aphrodite, the goddess of love, was often found by his side.

Aphrodite was married to Hephaestus, the god of blacksmiths and fire, but would rather have had Ares as her husband. She liked the fact that Ares was handsome and proud—qualities which her gentle husband did not possess. Hephaestus learned of the affair and decided to take revenge on them both.

Hephaestus fashioned a net and caught Ares and Aphrodite while they were in an intimate embrace. He then called all the Olympian gods over to see the captured pair. All the male gods laughed at the sight, saying that Aphrodite was so beautiful that they wished they were the ones caught in the net with her! The female deities refused to look at the sight, out of their own modesty.

In all, Aphrodite bore five children to Ares: Harmonia, Deimos and Phobos (Panic and Fear), Eros, the god of love, and Anteros, the god of mutual love or requited love.

In Battle

Aphrodite and Ares fought alongside the Trojans in the Trojan War. Since she was not accustomed to battle, Aphrodite was not a skilled or cunning warrior. The Greeks wounded her when she tried to defend her son, Aeneas. Aphrodite then fled to Mount Olympus, where her wounds were healed.

Ares was enraged when he saw his beloved Aphrodite hurt. He stormed down to Earth in his colossal war chariot, determined to punish the Greeks. When he got there, he stood by Hector, the greatest Trojan hero, and together they killed many Greek soldiers. The Greeks had Athena, the goddess of wisdom and just warfare—and Ares' old enemy—on their side. Because of this, they succeeded in wounding Ares, who then returned to Olympus wailing like a child. Aphrodite was there to comfort him.

Ares was always ready to pick a fight. He fought with Heracles twice to avenge the death of Cycnus, one of his mortal sons. In another story, Aphrodite became the lover of Adonis, the most beautiful of all young mortal men. Ares, mad with extreme jealousy, changed himself into a boar and killed Adonis. Such jealously and vengeance was typical of Ares.

FAMILY: Father was Zeus; mother was Hera; wife or paramour was Aphrodite.

IN ART: Ancient Greek art generally depicts Ares as armed and ready for battle. He is often shown wearing a plumed helmet and carrying a shield and spear. Ares has also been depicted with his wife, Aphrodite, and their son, Eros. In one famous statue, Ares is seated and the baby Eros is peeking out from behind his leg.

Many relief sculptures (sculptures carved on the sides of temples or other buildings) of ancient Greece depict Lapiths and Centaurs fight-

Ares, the god of war, was a fierce warrior. He is often described as being tall and handsome, but very vain. He took Aphrodite, goddess of love, as his lover, despite the fact that she was married to Hephaestus. Ares did not often care about the outcome of a war. He was primarily interested in the battle itself.

ing one another. Many of these sculptures were produced in the early fifth century B.C., at a time when the Greek city of Athens was at war with the Persians. The Lapiths were meant to represent the civilized Athenians, and the Centaurs—creatures who were half men, half horse—were meant to be the barbaric Persians.

IN LITERATURE: Ares appears in numerous Greek literary works. One of Greece's earliest known poets, Hesiod, wrote a description of how ancient Greeks would have imagined their god of war. In this scene, Cycnus, a son of Ares, has challenged the hero Heracles to a duel. This scene of Ares and Cycnus standing side-by-side illustrates the typical Greek conception of what Ares might have looked like:

> And [Heracles] slew Cycnus, the gallant son of Ares. For he found him in the close of far-shooting Apollo, him and his father Ares, never sated with war. Their armor shone like a flame of blazing fire

Ares (continued)

as they two stood in their car: their swift horses struck the earth and pawed it with their hoofs, and the dust rose like smoke about them, pounded by the chariot wheels and the horses' hoofs, while the well-made chariot and its rails rattled round them as the horses plunged.

> Hesiod, Shield of Heracles, lines 58–64, translation by Hugh G. Evelyn-White

From Homer, we know that the gods of Olympus—even Ares' father Zeus—hated Ares. In the *Iliad,* the Greek warrior Diomedes, with the help of Athena, engaged in single combat with Ares. Because Athena was helping him, Diomedes was able to avoid Ares' spear and ended up stabbing him in the belly. Ares immediately went up to Mount Olympus to complain to Zeus and told him that Athena was out of control. Zeus' response reveals just how much the gods disliked Ares:

> No longer come up to me and whine, you double-faced traitor! Of all the gods who dwell on Mount Olympus, you are the most hateful to me, with your constant love for strife and wars and battles. You get your temper from your mother, Hera, and it's uncontrollable. I myself can barely keep her in check with my threats. I suppose you have gotten this way through her instigations. But still, I cannot stand to see you enduring this anguish for so long. You are, after all, my son, and your mother bore you to me. But if you, with all your destructiveness, had been the child

of any other of the gods, you would long ago have been sent to a place far below all the gods of heaven.

> Homer, Iliad, book 5, lines 889–898, translation by Rick M. Newton

The *Homeric Hymn 8 to Ares* is one of the only works of ancient Greek literature that gives praise to the Greek god of war:

> Ares, exceeding in strength, chariot-rider, golden-helmed, doughty in heart, shield-bearer, Saviour of cities, harnessed in bronze, strong of arm, unwearying, mighty with the spear, O defence of Olympus, father of warlike Victory, ally of Themis, stern governor of the rebellious, leader of righteous men, sceptred King of manliness, who whirl your fiery sphere among the planets in their sevenfold courses through the aether wherein your blazing steeds ever bear you above the third firmament of heaven; hear me, helper of men, giver of dauntless youth!

> Homeric Hymn 8 to Ares, lines 1–9; translation by Hugh G. Evelyn-White

IN SPACE: The planet Mars is named for Ares' Roman equivalent, the god Mars. The planet has two small satellites, Phobos and Deimos, which are named after Ares' sons.

GO TO THE SOURCE: Ares appears in book 5 of Homer's *Iliad.* Homer also describes the love affair between Ares and Aphrodite in book 8 of the *Odyssey.* The worship of Ares is mentioned through-

out the *Histories* of Herodotus. Information on the god is also given in book 1 of Apollodorus's *Library.* There is also a poem, *Homeric Hymn to Ares,* which was written in the style of Homer and is one of the only examples of an ancient author giving praise to Ares. Most experts believe that the 34 *Homeric Hymns* were written several centuries after Homer lived.

Arethusa

Αρεθουσα

Arethusa (ahr-eh-THOO-suh) was a wood nymph and a close companion of Artemis, who was the Greek goddess of the hunt. A river god named Alpheus fell in love with Arethusa. One day, Alpheus came upon Arethusa bathing in a stream, and he chased after her. The pair ran and ran until they reached Delos, the birthplace of Artemis. The goddess came to Arethusa's rescue and changed her into a fountain. Alpheus did not want to give up his pursuit, though. He transformed himself into a river that flowed beneath the ocean from Greece to Delos. The waters of the river Alpheus joined the fountain of Arethusa. In this way, Alpheus was united forever with the object of his desire, Arethusa.

See also Alpheus.

Argo

Αργω

The *Argo* (AHR-goh) was the ship of the hero Jason. His companions were the Argonauts. Together they sailed in a quest to recover the Golden Fleece. The name *Argo* comes from the Greek word meaning "swift." The Greeks believed that the *Argo* was the first ship ever built. Even Homer's *Odyssey* refers to "the ship *Argo,* which everyone sings about." Although the *Argo* was very large, it moved gracefully across the waves. The mast of the ship was made from an oak tree from the forest of Dodona. The Dodona oaks had the power to see the future. Whenever he was in trouble, Jason sought advice from a sacred piece of oak built into the mast of the ship.

The *Argo* in the Stars

The ancient Greeks identified the *Argo* as a giant constellation in the skies of the Southern Hemisphere. Today, it is divided into four smaller constellations that make up different parts of the boat: Carina (keel), Puppis (stern), Pyxis (compass), and Vela (sails).

See also Argonauts; Golden Fleece; Jason.

In the photograph above, scientists from the Pacific Marine Enviromental Laboratory prepare an Argo float. The float works together with a space satellite to measure the temperature of Earth's oceans. It is named after the ship Jason used on his quest for the Golden Fleece.

In the drawing below, Athena is supervising the building of the Argo. The ship had a magical mast that could see the future.

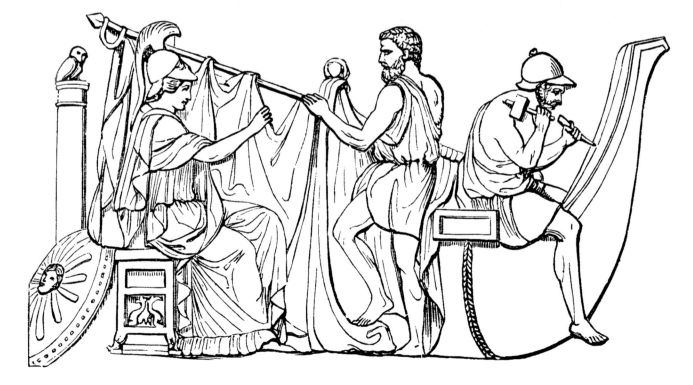

93

Argonauts

Αργοναυται

PRONUNCIATION: AHR-goh-nahts
CULTURE: Greek
ATTRIBUTES: Adventure

The Argonauts were the sailors of the ship, the *Argo*. The Greek hero, Jason, was their leader on a mission to win back the Golden Fleece.

The mythical adventure of Jason and the Argonauts took place in ancient times long before the Trojan War. The Argonauts accompanied the hero, Jason, on a quest to recover the Golden Fleece.

The Argonauts took their name from the *Argo,* their spectacular sailing ship. The *Argo,* built of oak under the supervision of the goddess Athena, had 50 pairs of oars. Among the 50 Argonauts were many Greek heroes: Admetus; Asclepius; Atalanta; Castor and Pollux and their cousins Idas and Lynceus; the winged heroes Calais and Zetes; Heracles; Hylas; Laertes; Meleager; Nestor; Orpheus; the prophets Mopsus and Idmon; Peleus; Philoctetes; and Telamon.

For the complete story of Jason and the Argonauts, *see* Jason.

IN ART: Though the individual adventures of the Argonauts were painted more often, there do exist

several representations of the group. A red figure vase now found at the Museum of Archeology in Florence, Italy, shows the group preparing for a fight. A fifth-century vase done by an artist known as the Niobid Painter is found in the Louvre Museum in Paris, France. It focuses on Heracles, but shows him surrounded by his compatriots, the Argonauts. The Italian artist Lorenzo Costa painted the Argonauts in their boat in his late fifteenth-century painting titled *The Journey of the Argonauts.* American artist and illustrator Maxfield Parrish created *The Argo.*

IN LITERATURE: In book 2 of his epic poem, *Paradise Lost,* seven-teenth-century English poet John Milton referred to the *Argo* in a scene describing extreme danger:

> And more endangered than when Argo passed
> Through Bosporus betwixt the justling rocks

William Shakespeare's *The Merchant of Venice* includes an allusion to the taking of the Golden Fleece by the Argonauts:

> Your mind is tossing on the ocean;
> There where your argosies, with portly sail
> Like signiors and rich burghers on the flood,
> Or as it were the pageants of the sea
> Do overpeer the petty traffickers,
> That curtsy to them, do them reverence,
> As they fly by them with their woven wings.

The painting to the left is by Maxfield Parrish (1870–1966). It shows the Argo sailing on the sea. The mythical adventure of Jason and the Argonauts took place in ancient times long before the Trojan War.

The Argonauts, pictured in the drawing below, were a group of young heroes who accompanied Jason in his quest for the Golden Fleece. In mythology, the Argo was the first boat ever built.

IN SPACE: Ancient people created a giant constellation, the *Argo,* in the skies of the Southern Hemisphere. Modern stargazers have divided the Argo constellation into four smaller constellations reflecting parts of the ship: Carina (Keel), Puppis (Stern), Pyxis (Compass), and Vela (Sails).

WORD HISTORY: *Argonaut* is another word for an adventurer.

MODERN USAGE: Some university sports teams have taken their names from the Jason myth. For example, the Argonauts take the field at both the College of Notre Dame in Florida and the University of West Florida.

GO TO THE SOURCE: The adventures of Jason and the Argonauts are chronicled in the *Argonautica* by Apollonius of Rhodes.

Argus

Αργος

PRONUNCIATION: AHR-guhs

EQUIVALENT CHARACTER: Argus was also known as *Panoptes* (all-seeing).

GENDER: Male

CULTURE: Greek

ATTRIBUTES: Vigilance

Argus was the trusted watchman of Hera, the queen of the gods. Argus's body was covered with 100 eyes. After Hermes killed Argus, Hera placed his eyes on the tail of the peacock so that he would never be forgotten.

Argus was a giant with 100 eyes covering his body. There are many tales of his fearlessness and strength. When Argus was young, he demonstrated his bravery by killing a bull that was ravaging the people of Arcadia, a region in Greece. Argus also killed Echidna, a monster who was half woman and half dragon.

Because of his bravery, Hera made Argus her personal watchman. With his 100 eyes, Argus was perfect for the job. When he slept, he never closed all of his eyes at the same time.

One day, Zeus, king of the gods, looked down to Earth. When his eyes fell on the beautiful mortal woman, Io, he fell hopelessly in love. Hiding himself in a rain cloud, Zeus went to her.

When Zeus' wife, Hera, looked down to Earth, she became suspicious when she saw the rain cloud hovering over the lovely Io. Just as Hera was about to discover them together, Zeus transformed Io into a small white cow.

But Hera was not so easily fooled. She knew the cow was really a woman. She begged Zeus to let her keep the cow. Not wanting to give himself away, Zeus agreed. Hera tied Io securely to a tree and assigned Argus to watch over her.

Zeus felt sorry for Io and longed to set her free. But Argus watched over Io night and day, never closing more than two of his eyes at one time. Zeus, still deeply in love, was determined to help Io. He sent Hermes, the cleverest of the Olympian gods, to set Io free.

Disguised as a shepherd and playing his panpipes, Hermes approached Argus. Argus, bored with his watchman's assignment, was glad to have some company while he guarded Io.

Hermes, playing a lilting tune on his panpipes, sat with Argus. Before long, Argus's eyes began to close, one by one. When all 100 eyes were closed Argus fell into a deep sleep. Hermes then dropped his panpipes and leaped up. With

TRUE OR FALSE?

1. Argus was a brave giant.
2. Argus did not know Hera, the Greek queen of the gods.
3. Hera assigned Argus to watch over a small white cow.
4. Panpipe music put Argus to sleep.
5. Hermes killed Argus.
6. The peacock's tail feathers have patterns that look like eyes in honor of Argus.

one stroke of his weapon, Hermes cut off Argus's head and set Io free.

Hera was heartbroken. She wanted to find a way to honor Argus's courage and loyalty. Hera gathered up all 100 of Argus's eyes and scattered them on the tail of her favorite bird, the peacock.

FAMILY: Father was Agenor.

IN ART: On ancient vase paintings, Argus was shown with his 100 eyes, but later artists rarely showed his many eyes. A popular scene for Modern painters is Hermes lulling Argus to sleep. The Spanish painter Diego Velazquez painted this scene in 1659; the

Italian Jacopo Amigoni in 1730, and the French artist Jean-Honore Fragonard in the late eighteenth century.

IN LITERATURE: Because the name Argus is associated with watchfulness, Odysseus in Homer's *Odyssey* named his watchdog Argus. Argus is mentioned in *The Knight's Tale*

According to the myth, Hermes lulled Argus, who had 100 eyes, to sleep and then killed him. Hera then put all of his eyes on the feathers of the peacock.

and *The Merchant's Tale,* both found within Geoffrey Chaucer's *Canterbury Tales.* In book 11 of the epic poem *Paradise Lost* by seventeenth-century English poet John Milton, the archangel Michael arrives to remove Adam and Eve from Eden with a host of cherubs whose bodies are:

> Spangled with eyes more
>   numerous than thos
> Of Argus, and more wakeful than
>   to drowse,
> Charmed with Arcadian pipe, the
>   pastoral ree
> Of Hermes, or his opiate rod

Argus appears in Elizabethan playwright William Shakespeare's *Love's Labour's Lost, The Merchant of Venice,* and *Troilus and Cressida.* In *The Merchant of Venice,* the character Portia alludes to Argus when she is telling someone to be watchful of her:

> Lie not a night from home; watch
>   me like Argus;
> If you do not, if I be left alone,
> Now by mine honour which is yet
>   mine own,
> I'll have that doctor for my
>   bedfellow.

In the popular *Harry Potter* novels written by J. K. Rowling, the caretaker and watchman of the Hogwarts School is named Argus Filch.

IN SPACE: Project Argus is the name for the SETI (Search for Extra-Terrestrial Intelligence) League's effort to coordinate roughly 5,000 small radio telescopes throughout the world to monitor for microwave signals of intelligent extraterrestrial origin.

IN SCIENCE: The Ohio State University in Columbus, Ohio, chose *Argus* for the name of a radio telescope that would be able to see in all directions at the same time, eliminating the need to point the telescope in one direction or another.

The butterfly, *Aricia Argus,* has eyelike spots on its wings. The Argus pheasant, found in Southeast Asia, has eyelike markings on its long tail.

WORD HISTORY: The adjective *Argus-eyed* refers to someone who is exceptionally alert and observant.

GO TO THE SOURCE: The death of Argus is recounted in book 1 of Ovid's *Metamorphoses.*

Ariadne

Αριαδνη

PRONUNCIATION: air-ee-AD-nee
GENDER: Female
CULTURE: Greek
ATTRIBUTES: Helped Theseus escape from the Labyrinth.

Ariadne was the beautiful daughter of King Minos and Queen Pasiphae of Crete. Ariadne met Theseus when he was sent to be food for the monstrous Minotaur. She fell in love with Theseus. Ariadne gave Theseus a ball of magic golden thread, which he used to escape from the Labyrinth, home of the Minotaur. Ariadne left with Theseus for Athens, but he abandoned her before they arrived in Athens and before they were married. She eventually married Dionysus, the Greek god of wine.

Ariadne was the daughter of Minos, king of Crete, and his wife, Queen Pasiphae. One day King Minos angered Poseidon, god of the sea. The god punished Minos by driving Queen Pasiphae mad. Pasiphae fell in love with a bull and the two had a monster baby, the Minotaur.

The Minotaur had the body of a human and the head of a bull. It was kept in an elaborate maze called the Labyrinth. Every nine years, fourteen young men and women from Athens were given as sacrifice to feed this terrible beast.

Ariadne was one of the daughters of Minos and Pasiphae. She lived in Crete with her parents and witnessed the sacrifice of the fourteen young people to the Minotaur every nine years. When it was time again to offer the sacrifices to the Minotaur, Ariadne watched for the arrival of the fourteen young people. When they arrived there was a beautiful young man among them. His name was Theseus and he was a prince of Athens. Ariadne fell in love with him and could not bear the thought of him being fed to the Minotaur. She decided to help him slay the Minotaur and escape his fate.

Ariadne Helps Theseus

The love-struck Ariadne went to Theseus. She offered to help him if he promised to marry her and take her with him when he returned to Athens. Theseus wanted more than anything to escape being sacrificed. He agreed to marry Ariadne if he survived his encounter with the Minotaur.

The night before Theseus was supposed to be thrown into the Labyrinth, Ariadne crept to his jail cell. She presented him with a ball of magic golden thread, saying it would show him the way to the Minotaur.

The next morning, Theseus was led from his jail cell and thrown into the mouth of the Labyrinth.

TRUE OR FALSE?

1. Ariadne's father was the king of Ethiopia.
2. Ariadne loved the Greek hero Theseus.
3. Theseus received a ball of magic golden thread from Ariadne.
4. Ariadne and Theseus were married and lived happily in Crete.

Ariadne and Theseus

A play adapted from *Plays from the Wonder-Book and Tanglewood Tales* by Grace Dietrich McCarthy, Boston: Educational Publishing Company, 1910.

CHARACTERS

NARRATOR

AETHRA, *former wife of King Aegeus*

THESEUS, *their son*

AEGEUS, *king of Athens*

PALLANTIDS, *sons of Pallas, the brother of Aegeus*

MEDEA, *current wife of King Aegeus*

MESSENGER *from Crete*

MINOS, *king of Crete*

ARIADNE, *his daughter*

GUARD *at the palace of Minos*

CHORUS/COURTIERS

The narrator sits on a stool on the side of the stage.

The student playing the role of Theseus will need a sword and a pair of sandals.

The character of Ariadne will need to give Theseus a sword and a spool of thread.

The chorus can be made up of courtiers in the palace of Aegeus.

PROLOGUE

Narrator: Once there lived a woman named Aethra, who bore a son named Theseus, but was abandoned by her husband, Aegeus. Before he left, Aegeus left something for his son: items buried beneath a huge rock. Theseus would have to be strong before he could find out what was underneath. As he grew, Theseus excelled at athletics. He tried every year to lift the rock at his mother's request; finally, after three years of trying, Theseus succeeded, Beneath the rock he found a bronze sword and a pair of golden sandals. His mother tried to explain to him that they would lead him to his destiny—to meet his father and to become a hero.

ACT I

(The house of AETHRA in the city of Troezen)

Aethra: Theseus, my son, come with me where we can look out at the sea. *(They go outside and look down upon the sea)* Do you see the land below?

Theseus: Yes, it is the city of Troezen, where I was born and raised.

Aethra: It is but a little land, barren and rocky, and looks towards the bleak northeast. Do you see that land beyond?

Theseus: Yes, that is Athens.

Aethra: That is a beautiful and large land, Theseus, and it looks toward the sunny south. It is a land of olive oil and honey—the joy of gods and men. The gods have blessed it with mountains, run through with marble and silver; the hills are sweet with thyme and basil; the meadows smell of violets; and the nightingales sing all day in the thickets by the side of flowing streams. What would you do, Theseus, if you were king of such a land?

Theseus: If I were king of such a land, I would rule it wisely and well, so that when I died all men might weep over my tomb.

Aethra: Then take this sword and these sandals, and go to Aegeus, king of Athens, who lives on Pallas's hill, and present yourself to your father.

Theseus: (weeping) Must I leave you, my mother?

Chorus: Don't cry, Theseus. Your mother has dealt all her life with sorrow and can live with the sadness of losing you, knowing you will one day become a great hero.

(Exit all)

ACT II

(THESEUS arrives at the palace of King Aegeus in Athens, having traveled for many weeks to reach the city and having met and destroyed many savages and evil-doers. He speaks to a group of young men.)

Pallantids: Hello, stranger. What is your will today?

Theseus: I have come to ask for hospitality.

Pallantids: Then take it, and welcome. You look like a hero and a bold warrior, and we welcome you to drink with us.

Theseus: I ask no hospitality of you, I ask it of Aegeus, the king and master of this house.

Pallantids: We are all masters here.

Theseus: Then I am master as much as the rest of you. *(He strides in and looks around)*

Pallantids: *(Aside, to the audience)* This is an arrogant fellow! We ought to throw him out.

Theseus: Go tell King Aegeus, your master, that Theseus of Troezen is here, and asks to be his guest awhile. *(The* PALLANTIDS *depart)*

Chorus: The sons of Pallus are angry! They are threatened by this brave stranger. They don't know it, but he is their cousin, and rightful heir to the throne of Athens.

(Enter KING AEGEUS*)*

Aegeus: Where is this Theseus? Are you the hero who has rid the country from many monsters?

Theseus: I have delivered the king's realm from many monsters; therefore I have come to ask for a reward.

Aegeus: It is little that I can give you, noble lad, and nothing that is worthy of you. If the tales I hear are true then surely you are no mortal man, or at least no mortal's son.

Theseus: All I ask is to eat and drink at your table.

Aegeus: That I can give you, since I am master of my own hall. Put a seat for Theseus and set before him the best of the feast.

(Enter MEDEA, *with a cup of wine)*

Medea: How Aegeus welcomed this lad from Troezen! He welcomes him too warmly for him to be a stranger; perhaps he is closer to Aegeus already than anyone knows. What if he is to become master here? *(She hands* THESEUS *a glass of wine)* Drink, hero, of my charmed cup, which gives rest after great work and worry, which heals all wounds, and which renews energy. Drink of my cup.

Chorus: Beware Theseus! Medea seeks to poison you to make sure you don't stand in the way of her own child becoming heir to the Athenian throne. Do not drink from her cup!

Theseus: The wine is rich and fragrant and you—the wine bearer—are as fair as the gods. But first pledge yourself to me and drink from your own cup—the wine will be sweeter from your lips.

Medea: (turning pale and stammering) Forgive me, fair hero, but I am ill, and should not drink any wine.

Theseus: You will drink from that cup or die. *(Lifts up his sword; MEDEA throws the cup on the ground and dashes out)*

Aegeus: What have you done?

Theseus: I have rid the land of an enchantment—that wine was poisoned. *(Showing sword and sandals)* I am to show you these, Sire.

Aegeus: (turning to the people) My son, my son! Behold my son, a better man than his father was before him.

Pallantids: Why should we welcome this stranger? We don't even know where he comes from.

Theseus: (draws his sword) Go in peace, if you will, my cousins; if not you take your life into your own hands. *(Going back to Aegeus)* Why do you weep and turn away from me?

Aegeus: You will know soon, my son. I hear the messenger at the door.

(Enter MESSENGER)

Messenger: People and king of Athens, where is your yearly tribute? *(The people moan)*

Theseus: Who are you, you dog, who dare demand such payment here?

Messenger: I am not a dog. My master, Minos, king of Crete and wisest of kings on Earth, has sent me here to do his bidding. Surely you must be a stranger here, or you would know why I have come, and that I come by right.

Theseus: I am a stranger here. Tell me, then, why you come.

Messenger: I am here to fetch the payment that King Aegeus owes to Minos, conqueror of this land. Minos mourns the death of his son, Androgeus, who came to Athens to take part in the Olympic games and who won every event he entered. The people here honored him as a hero, but Aegeus envied him and plotted to kill him. So Minos came and avenged his son, and would not leave until he was promised a yearly payment: seven young men and seven young girls, who return with me to Crete in a ship with black sails.

Theseus: I should kill you for saying such things! Father, tell me the truth.

Aegeus: Blood was shed in the land unjustly, and by blood it is avenged. Don't break my heart with questions; it is enough to endure in silence. *(THESEUS groans)*

Theseus: I will go myself with these boys and girls, and kill Minos upon his royal throne.

Aegeus: You shall not go, my son. I look to you to rule these people after I am dead and gone. You shall not go to die horribly as those boys and girls do; Minos thrusts them into the Labyrinth that houses the Minotaur—a monster who eats them alive.

Theseus: That's even more reason why I should go and kill the beast. Have I not killed all evil-doers and monsters so that this land is free? This Minotaur shall have the same fate—and Minos as well, if he dares to prevent me.

Aegeus: But how would you kill him, my son? All are thrown into the Labyrinth naked and defenseless—you would not have your club or your armor.

Theseus: I have my fists and my teeth; and are there no stones in that Labyrinth?

Aegeus: (clinging to him) If you must go, my son, go! But promise me but this—if you are, by some miracle, able to return, take down the black sail of the ship and replace it with a white one, so that I know you are safe.

Theseus: (to the Messenger) I choose to be one of the seven.

Messenger: Are you sure you know what you are doing?

Theseus: I know. Let us go down to the black-sailed ship.

Chorus: Brave Theseus! He selflessly puts himself in danger to mend the strife between Athens and Crete, and to save the doomed young men and women who would be the Minotaur's supper!

ACT III

(THESEUS *stands before King Minos in his palace in Crete*)

Theseus: I ask a favor, King Minos. Let me be the first thrown to the beast. I have come here by my own choice, unlike these other boys, and so deserve to go before them.

Minos: Who are you, brave youth?

Theseus: I am the son of Aegeus—the man you hate more than anyone—and I've come here to settle this matter once and for all.

Minos: You mean to die to atone for your father's sin. No—go back in peace, my son. It is a pity that one so brave should die.

Theseus: I have sworn that I will not go back until I have seen the monster face to face.

Minos: (frowning) Then you shall see him! Take this madman away!

(*Enter* ARIADNE)

Ariadne: It is too sad that a man such as you should die! Quick, get back to your ship at once, for I have bribed the guards outside the door. Escape, you and all your friends, and go back in peace to Greece. Only take me with you! I dare not stay after you are gone, for my father would kill me if he found out what I have done.

Theseus: I cannot go home in peace until I have killed the Minotaur and avenged the deaths of all the young men and women who have been sacrificed.

Ariadne: But how will you kill the Minotaur?

Theseus: I don't know and I don't care, but I will find a way.

Ariadne: If you do succeed in killing him, how will you find your way out of the Labyrinth?

Theseus: I don't know that either and I don't care.

Ariadne: You are so brave! But I can still help you—I will give you a sword to kill the beast, and a spool of thread, so that you might find your way out again. Only promise me, that if you escape safely, you will take me home with you to Greece, for my father will surely kill me if he knows what I have done.

(*Enter* GUARD)

Guard: You are ordered to the Labyrinth.

(*He leads Theseus away*)

ACT IV

(THESEUS *and* ARIADNE *talk quietly outside the entrance to the labyrinth*)

Theseus: It is done.

Ariadne: Is the monster dead?

Theseus: He is dead.

Ariadne: Tell me what happened. Are you hurt?

Theseus: I wound my way through the Labyrinth, leaving a trail of thread behind me from your spool. At last I met the Minotaur in a narrow passage. I have never seen anything so strange! He had a man's body, a bull's head, and the teeth of a lion. He tried to charge me, but I jumped aside and cut his leg as he ran past. I chased him as he ran, stabbing him from behind, still remembering to let out thread from the spool as I went. At last I caught him by his horns and drove the sword into his throat. Then I found my way back, feeling the path of the thread, until I came to the entrance and saw you waiting for me.

Ariadne: So it is done. There is no time to lose— we must be quick and set the prisoners free while the guard sleeps. Then we will hurry to the ship together, hoist the sail, and escape.

EPILOGUE

Narrator: And so it went that brave Theseus, who cared more for his country than for himself, conquered the fierce Minotaur and set sail for Greece. He was accompanied by the young men and women he spared from the yearly sacrifice, as well as Ariadne, who went against her father to help Theseus. He would return to Athens to succeed his father as king.

While Ariadne was sleeping, Theseus abandoned her. Later Dionysus presented her with jewels, which are memorialized in the skies as the constellation, Corona Borealis.

Concealed in his garments was the ball of magic golden thread. He tied one end of the thread to a column, as Ariadne had instructed him. The golden thread began to unwind, showing Theseus the way into the Labyrinth.

When Theseus found the Minotaur, he fought him bravely and was victorious. The Minotaur was dead! But now Theseus was stuck in the Labyrinth. In the excitement of his battle with the Minotaur, Theseus had forgotten about the golden thread. He looked around and found the trail of thread. Inch by inch and step by step Theseus followed the golden thread all the way back to the entrance of the Labyrinth.

The Bride of Dionysus

Theseus and Ariadne happily left Crete together, but she never made it to Athens. Dionysus, the Greek god of wine, appeared to Theseus in a dream and told him to leave Ariadne on the island of Naxos. Dionysus had chosen Ariadne to be his bride, and he did not want Theseus to marry her first. Theseus, afraid to disobey a god, had no choice but to take Ariadne to Naxos.

When their ship landed on Naxos, the passengers, including Theseus and Ariadne, enjoyed a picnic on the beach. After finishing the big meal, Ariadne went to rest in the shade of a large tree. When she began to sleep soundly, Theseus saw his chance to escape. He quietly ordered the other passengers to return to ship, and they sailed away.

When Ariadne awoke, she was terrified to find that she was alone. She wept for Theseus and cried out for him to return. Moments later,

Dionysus appeared to her. He was followed by a band of maenads and satyrs, his most loyal followers. Dionysus dried Ariadne's tears and gave her sparkling jewels and a cup of dark wine. When the wine touched her lips, a smile broke over her face. At that moment, Ariadne fell in love with Dionysus. She forgot Theseus completely.

Dionysus and Ariadne lived happily together for many years. When she died, Dionysus took her jewels and placed them in the sky as a constellation, so that his beautiful wife would never be forgotten.

FAMILY: Father was Minos; mother was Pasiphae; husband was Dionysus.

IN ART: Many ancient Greek vase paintings include Ariadne. She is often depicted alongside her immortal husband Dionysus, the Greek god of wine. The two are sometimes represented riding in a chariot. Several vase paintings depict the scene where Dionysus presented jewels to Ariadne. In one, Ariadne supports a drunken Dionysus. In another, the luxurious married life of Ariadne and Dionysus is depicted. The couple reclines on a couch drinking wine served to them by one of Dionysus's loyal satyrs.

Many sculptures exist from classical and modern times depicting Dionysus (or Bacchus, his equivalent in Roman mythology) with Ariadne. One of the most famous paintings from the Renaissance is entitled *Bacchus and Ariadne*. It was painted from 1523–24 by the Venetian artist Titian and depicts a frightened Ariadne at the very left. Bacchus, the Roman equivalent of the Greek god Dionysus, is leaping out of his chariot to claim her as his wife. The image of Theseus's ship sailing away can be seen in the background.

IN LITERATURE: Ariadne appears in William Shakespeare's play *Two Gentlemen of Verona*. Shakespeare alludes to Theseus's abandonment of Ariadne:

> Madam, 'twas Ariadne passioning
> For Theseus' perjury and unjust
>   flight.
> *Act IV scene 4, lines 171–172*

Shakespeare talks about Ariadne again in *A Midsummer Night's Dream* when Oberon accuses his wife Titania of abandoning him:

> How canst thou thus, for shame,
>   Titania,
> Glance at my credit with Hippolyta
> Knowing I know thy love to
>   Theseus?
> Didst not thou lead him through
>   the glimmering night
> From Perigenia, whom he ravish'd?
> And make him with fair Aegle
>   break his faith,
> With Ariadne and Antiope?
> *Act II scene 1, lines 74–80*

Corona Borealis: The Northern Crown

Corona Borealis represents the crown or necklace of Princess Ariadne.

Dionysus, the god of wine, placed this constellation in the sky so that no one would ever forget Ariadne. Some Greeks, however, thought that this constellation represented the ball of thread that Ariadne gave to Theseus to help him escape from the Labyrinth.

The ancient Persians, on the other hand, saw a broken platter, since the constellation is formed by an incomplete ring of stars.

The brightest star in Corona Borealis is (1) Alphecca. It is located in the middle of the semicircle that forms Corona Borealis. Alphecca is around 75 light-years from Earth, and is about 60 times brighter than the Sun.

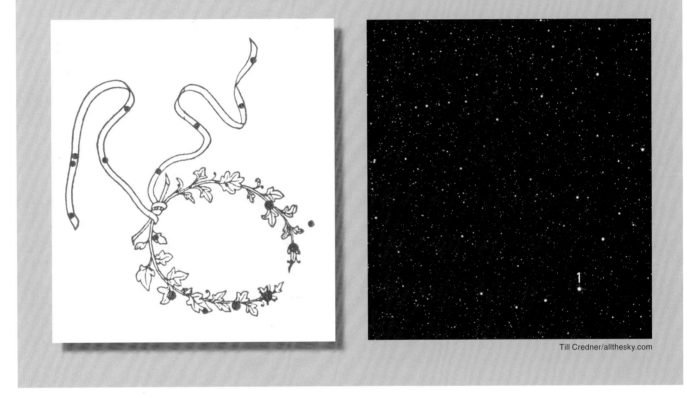

Till Credner/allthesky.com

IN SPACE: The Corona Borealis, or Northern Crown, is a constellation formed by a group of stars in a semicircular arc. This constellation represents the jewels given to Ariadne by Dionysus. After Ariadne's death, Dionysus placed this constellation in the heavens so that she would never be forgotten.

MODERN USAGE: Nineteenth-century German composer Richard Strauss wrote an opera entitled *Ariadne auf Naxos*. It recounts the story of Ariadne's abandonment by Theseus on the island of Naxos.

Ariadne Island and Ariadne Cove can both be found on the southern coast of Alaska.

The English phrase "clue of Ariadne" refers to the ball of thread that Ariadne gave to Theseus to help him escape from the labyrinth. One meaning of the English word "clue" is "thread," although it is not commonly used with that meaning today. When someone is able to solve a puzzling mystery or dense problem, we say that he or she has found the clue of Ariadne.

GO TO THE SOURCE: Ariadne and the story of the Labyrinth can be found in book 8 of the *Metamorphoses* by Ovid. The story of how Ariadne helped Theseus and was then abandoned by him can be found in the *Life of Theseus* of Plutarch and in books 7 and 8 of Ovid's *Metamorphoses*. A poem by the Roman poet Catullus,

Arion was a singer who enchanted dolphins with his music. This photograph shows that the name Arion continues to resonate in American history.

the *Epithalamium,* celebrates the occasion when she awoke on Naxos to find Dionysus in front of her. In that poem, Ariadne laments over Theseus's forgetfulness and curses him so that he will later forget to change the sails on his ship.

See also Aegeus.

Arion

Αριων

Arion (AIR-ee-uhn) was a bard (singer) in Greek mythology. He lived in the court of Periander, the king of Corinth. One day, Arion sailed to Sicily to compete in a musical contest. To his delight, he won first prize—a rather large sum of money. On his way home, the crew of the ship threatened to kill him and take his prize money. Arion offered to give up the money in exchange for his life, but the crew feared that he would turn them over to Periander.

Arion made one last bargain with the crew: He told them that he would willingly throw himself overboard if he were allowed to sing his own death song. The crew agreed, and Arion, dressed in his singer's costume, stood at the edge of the ship and sang. His song was so enchanting that the dolphins in the sea gathered around the ship to hear it. When Arion finished his song and jumped into the sea,

the dolphins took him up on their backs and carried him safely to shore.

It is interesting to note that, in the version of the story told by Herodotus (book 1 of the *Histories*), Arion sings his song in a shrill voice. Some scholars suggest that the dolphins that rescued Arion came in response to his high-pitched voice. Today, dolphin trainers use whistles that are so high-pitched that human ears cannot hear them, but dolphins can.

Aristophanes

Αριστοφανης

The Greek dramatist Aristophanes (c. 445–c. 385 B.C.) was born in Athens. He was so young when he began writing that his first plays were submitted in competitions under another name because he was not old enough to contend for the prize. He wrote about 54 comedies throughout his life, but only 11 have survived. *Lysistrata* and *The Clouds* are among his most admired pieces; others are *The Wasps, The Birds,* and *The Frogs.*

Aristophanes was politically conservative; he mercilessly mocked the newer movements in politics and thought. One of his finest plays, *The Clouds,* is a satire against the famous Greek philosopher Socrates. His plays contain passages of beautiful poetry and sparkling wit, as well as much obscene humor.

Artemis

Άρτεμις

PRONUNCIATION: AHR-tuh-mihs
EQUIVALENT CHARACTER: The Roman
    goddess Diana
GENDER: Female
CULTURE: Greek
ATTRIBUTES: Hunting; the Forest;
    Chastity; the Moon

Artemis was the Greek goddess of the hunt. She also protected the forest and the animals that lived there. As a young girl, Zeus granted Artemis's greatest wish: that she would never have to marry. She much preferred to hunt with her pack of hunting dogs. Artemis is often represented by a stag, but she has also been depicted with bears, boars, goats, and lions. She is often called "Mistress of the Wild Animals." Her silver bow and arrows brought painless death to whomever they pierced.

Artemis was the daughter of Zeus, the king of the Olympian gods. Her mother was Leto, a mortal woman. The two met when Zeus looked down on the Earth and saw the beautiful Leto. She was a daughter of the Titan Coeus. Zeus fell in love with Leto and decided he wanted to be with her. Zeus was already married to Hera, queen of the gods. He knew that Hera would be jealous of his love for Leto. In an effort to keep his love for Leto a secret, Zeus transformed himself and Leto into quails. Not long after that, Leto became pregnant.

As with all his other love affairs, Zeus was not able to deceive Hera. Hera was furious when she learned of Leto's pregnancy. Hera declared that Leto would not be able to give birth in any place the Sun shone. She even prevented her daughter Ilithyia, the goddess of childbirth, from helping Leto.

A Gift for Delos

Leto was distraught, and wandered all over Greece looking for a place to give birth to her children. No one welcomed her, for they feared Hera's wrath. Leto finally arrived at the island of Delos, which was so new that it floated on top of the sea. The people who lived there welcomed Leto, and in the shade of a palm tree she gave birth to the divine twin children of Zeus. First was Artemis, a beautiful daughter with hair as black as night. Within minutes of her birth, Artemis

Artemis was the goddess of the hunt and wild animals. Her hunting bows were made by Hephaestus and the Cyclopes.

helped her mother give birth to her twin brother, Apollo.

Zeus was overjoyed that Leto had given him such radiant children. Zeus brought Leto and the twin babies up to Mount Olympus to live among the gods. Artemis became the goddess of the hunt and of all wild animals, while Apollo became the god of light, music, poetry, and reason.

Artemis's Wish

When she was still a very young child, Artemis asked Zeus to make her a promise. Zeus could not refuse his daughter, and he swore on the River Styx that he would grant her whatever she asked for. Artemis requested that she never be forced to marry. Zeus granted this wish, leaving Artemis free to hunt as much as she wanted. He also gave her a silver bow with silver arrows, a pack of hunting dogs, and a group of forest nymphs to be her attendants.

From that point on, Artemis hunted whenever she pleased. Her silver arrows were magic and instantly killed whatever they hit. Since Artemis was a protector of women, her arrows often brought

Artemis (continued)

painless death to women. Artemis also enjoyed dancing and bathing with her nymph followers.

Artemis was also the goddess of nature. She kept careful watch over all animals and the forests and meadows they lived in. The deer and the bear were the animals most sacred to her. Artemis could be seen driving through the forest in her chariot drawn by four deer with golden antlers.

A Vengeful Goddess

Artemis was quick to punish any mortal who offended her. One night after a long and successful hunt, Artemis and her nymphs found a spring in the forest and decided to bathe in it. At that very moment, Actaeon, a mortal who was out hunting with his hounds, stumbled across the very pool where Artemis was bathing.

Artemis became infuriated when she saw Actaeon looking at her exposed body. Her nymphs tried to hide her, but it was no use; Artemis towered over them. In her anger, Artemis flung a handful of water at Actaeon. Within a few moments, Actaeon transformed into a deer. He was torn apart by his own hounds, which no longer recognized him.

Artemis also proved to be a vengeful goddess in the story of Niobe, the arrogant mortal queen of Thebes. One day, Niobe declared to the Theban people that she was happier than Leto, the mother of Artemis and Apollo. Niobe also tried to convince her people that she was superior to Leto because she had seven beautiful daughters and seven handsome sons, while Leto had only one of each.

Artemis and Apollo were furious, for it was a great offense for mortals to compare themselves to the gods. In their anger, the twin gods descended to Earth to take revenge on Niobe. Artemis shot Niobe's daughters with her silver arrows, killing them instantly and painlessly, while Apollo killed her sons with his piercing golden arrows. It was only after all her children were dead that Niobe showed regret for insulting the gods. In her grief, Niobe wept for countless days and weeks until Zeus took pity on her and turned her to stone. However, her sorrow was so great that the rock continued to weep for all eternity.

A Love Lost

Many other stories depict the vengeance of Artemis. She once became angry with Orion, a son of Poseidon who could walk on water. Even though Artemis hated most men, the handsome Orion was such a gifted hunter that he became one of her favorite hunting companions. She even fell in love with him. When Artemis discovered that he was in love with Eos, the goddess of dawn, she went into a jealous rage and shot Orion with her arrows. Artemis also took revenge on King Oineus of Calydon because he offered sacrifices to all gods, but he had forgotten to sacrifice to her. As punishment, she sent the Calydonian boar to ravage his kingdom.

Hera Tricks Artemis

There were also times when Artemis took revenge by accident, as in the story of Callisto. At one time, Callisto was one of the nymphs who followed Artemis. When Zeus saw Callisto, he fell in love with her (as he often did). The two became lovers. In order to hide Callisto from his wife Hera, Zeus transformed her into a bear. Hera knew what Zeus had done, and she wanted to take revenge on him. Hera challenged Artemis to kill the bear. Artemis did not suspect that the bear was really Callisto. Hera knew Artemis loved to hunt, and Artemis shot the bear with her arrows. Zeus was the only one who knew the bear was Callisto. He took Callisto's body and hung it in the sky as the bear constellation, Ursa Major.

Artemis Takes Sides in the Trojan War

The vengeance of Artemis also played a role in the Trojan War. King Agamemnon of Mycenae, the commander of the Greek forces, ordered all the chiefs to assemble their armies at the city of Aulis on the eastern coast of Greece. While at Aulis, Agamemnon killed a deer that was sacred to Artemis.

Artemis was angry and she wanted to punish Agamemnon. First, she sent a plague to ravage the Greek army. Then she calmed the waters and winds so that none of their ships could sail.

Agamemnon did not know what to do to appease Artemis's anger. He asked a soothsayer for advice. The soothsayer told Agamemnon to sacrifice his daughter Iphigenia to the goddess. If he did so, Artemis would lift the plague and send Winds so the ships could sail.

By the time Iphigenia was about to be killed, Artemis had calmed down. In the version recounted by Euripides, Artemis could not bear to see the young girl lose her life, so Artemis rescued her and left a deer to be sacrificed in her place. Artemis carried the young girl to the island of Tauris, where Iphigenia became her head priestess. When the Greeks finally arrived at Troy, Artemis fought alongside the Trojans with her brother Apollo. In the version recounted by Aeschylus, however, Artemis does not rescue Iphigenia.

Agamemnon brutally slays his own daughter.

Artemis Is Worshiped Throughout Greece

Artemis's most devout worshipers could be found throughout Greece: on the island of Delos where she was born; in the lands of Arcadia,

Artemis (continued)

where her favorite hunting spots were; and in other Greek cities such as Athens and Brauron. In Arcadia, her priests and priestesses were bound by an oath to live pure and chaste lives. In Athens, 500 goats were sacrificed to Artemis every year in celebration of their victory at Marathon over the Persians.

Some of her most devout followers lived in the city of Brauron, just east of Athens. The citizens of Brauron had once accidentally killed a bear that was sacred to Artemis. In order to soothe the goddess's anger, they started holding yearly celebrations in her honor. During the festivals, the youngest girls would dress themselves in bearskins and dance like bears. The most devoted follower of Artemis was a man named Hippolytus, who admired Artemis for her chastity.

See also Diana; Luna; Hecate; Actaeon; Niobe; Orion; Meleager; Atalanta; Callisto; Agamemnon; Iphigenia.

FAMILY: Father was Zeus; mother was Leto; twin brother was Apollo.

IN ART: Artemis appears in many ancient vase paintings. Some ancient artists showed Artemis dressed as a huntress, wearing a short robe and armed with quiver and bow. In other ancient depic-tions, Artemis appears as a moon goddess, dressed in a long, flowing gown and holding a torch. In every work of art she is seen as beautiful, youthful, and energetic.

In an ancient relief sculpture from the Temple of Artemis at Brauron, Artemis sits with a stag right next to her. (A relief sculpture is a type of art used to decorate walls. Three-dimensional figures appear to come out of a flat background.) The goddess and the stag appear to be staring at each other, but the stag shows no fear of Artemis, the huntress. The sculptor probably intended to represent Artemis as the patron goddess of forest animals.

The temple of Artemis at Ephesus, built around 550 B.C., is one of the Seven Wonders of the Ancient World. Several artists created bronze sculptures to decorate the huge marble temple, which measured 400 feet (120 meters) by 200 feet (60 meters). An estimated 127 marble columns, each 66 feet (20 meters) tall, supported the tile roof. A large statue of Artemis stood in the center of the temple. The statue depicted the goddess with numerous sacred animals—including lions, deer, rams, and bulls—around her head and on her legs.

The original temple at Ephesus was destroyed by fire in 356 B.C., but another temple was built in its place. Sections of the second temple were recovered and taken to the British Museum in London, England, where they are displayed. The temple foundation remains near modern-day Ephesus. Only a single column has been restored.

IN LITERATURE: A description of Artemis is given in the *Homeric Hymn 27 to Artemis* from ancient Greece. Although this poem is attributed to Homer, the true author is unknown. In this passage, Artemis has golden arrows instead of silver ones, and her brother Apollo is referred to as Phoebus Apollo:

> I sing of Artemis, whose shafts are of gold, who cheers on the hounds, the pure maiden, shooter of stags, who delights in archery, own sister to Apollo with the golden sword.
>
> Over the shadowy hills and windy peaks she draws her golden bow, rejoicing in the chase, and sends out grievous shafts…
>
> But the goddess with a bold heart turns every way destroying the race of wild beasts: and when she is satisfied and has cheered her heart, this huntress who delights in arrows slackens her supple bow and goes to the great house of her dear brother Phoebus Apollo.
>
> Homeric Hymn 27 to Artemis, *lines 1–6, 11–14; translation by Hugh G. Evelyn-White*

In Homer's *Odyssey*, Odysseus meets a princess named Nausicaa, whose beauty is compared to Artemis:

> As Artemis, who rejoices in her arrows, makes her way in the mountains…and delights in wild boars and swift deer, and her nymphs attend her, the daughters of aegis-bearing Zeus, as they roam the fields and play. Leto delights in her heart, as her daughter stands out a head taller than all the others and is easily the most beautiful of all the fair nymphs. In this way did the young girl shine among her maidservants.

Homer, Odyssey, book 6, lines 102–109; translation by Rick M. Newton

IN SPACE: Artemis Chasma is a sunken trench on the planet Venus. It is a vast circular region

The Romans built temples to Artemis throughout their empire. The ruins of this temple of Artemis stand in modern-day Jordan.

with a diameter of over 1500 miles (2400 kilometers). From the lowest point to the highest point, Artemis Chasma is about 4.5 miles (7 kilometers) deep.

WORD HISTORY: *Artemisia* is a plant genus that includes wormwood, mugwort, and sagebrush, among others. Many of the plants in this genus have white or silver hairs on their leaves, which are said to reflect moonlight. These plants grow only in the Northern Hemisphere and can generally be found in drier climates. Most plants in the *Artemisia* genus have aromatic leaves or flowers, and some—such as tarragon—are grown as herbs for cooking.

GO TO THE SOURCE: Artemis is mentioned in the works of almost every ancient Greek author. Information on Artemis can be found throughout the *Library* and *Epitome* by Apollodorus. Information on the ways in which people worshiped the goddess can be found in *Description of Greece* by Pausanias and in the *History* of Herodotus. She is also mentioned in Hesiod's *Theogony,* and in many Homeric poems. In addition to the *Iliad* and the *Odyssey,* two *Homeric Hymns* are dedicated to Artemis. (There are 34 *Homeric Hymns* that most experts believe were written several centuries after Homer lived.)

In Euripides' play *Hippolytus,* the goddess of love Aphrodite punishes Hippolytus because of his devotion to chaste and pure Artemis. Artemis was also mentioned in other plays by Euripides, including *The Phoenician Women, Iphigenia at Aulis,* and *Iphigenia Among the Taurians.* The tragic playwrights Aeschylus and Sophocles also mention Artemis in their plays, as does the comic playwright Aristophanes.

Ophiuchus: The Serpent Bearer

Ophiuchus is pictured grasping Serpens, the snake. The head of the snake is called *Serpens caput*, and is located to the east of Ophiuchus. To the west is the serpent's tail, *Serpens cauda*.

The ancient Greeks believed that this constellation was a depiction of Asclepius, the god of healing and medicine. The snake was a symbol of health in the ancient world. The staff of Asclepius, known as the *caduceus*, was a rod with two snakes wrapped around it. This is still a symbol for doctors in the modern world.

In the Northern Hemisphere, Ophiuchus is visible from May to September. It is generally visible from anywhere that is far from the Earth's poles. In the Southern Hemisphere this is a winter constellation.

Ophiuchus reaches its highest point in the sky near the beginning of June.

The brightest star in Ophiuchus is (1) Ras Alhague. This star marks the location of the serpent bearer's head. Ras Alhague is 47 light-years from Earth, and is about 25 times brighter than the Sun.

In Arabic, the word *ophiuchus* means "head of the serpent bearer."

Till Credner/allthesky.com

114

Asclepius

Ασκληπιος

PRONUNCIATION: eh-SKLAY-pee-uhs
EQUIVALENT CHARACTER: The Roman god Aesculapius
GENDER: Male
CULTURE: Greek
ATTRIBUTES: Healing; Medicine

Asclepius was a mortal doctor who could bring the dead back to life. After his death, Asclepius became the god of healing and medicine. His emblem was the physician's staff with two snakes wrapped around it.

Asclepius was one of the greatest doctors in ancient Greece. He was a mortal, but his father was Apollo, the god of light, music, and poetry. Asclepius got his mortality from his mortal mother, Coronis. In Greek mythology, he was known as the doctor who could bring the dead back to life. After his death, Asclepius became the god of healing and medicine.

Asclepius's mother Coronis had agreed to marry the god Apollo, even though she was truly in love with Ischys, another mortal. One day, a white crow came to Apollo and told him that Coronis was planning to run off with Ischys. Apollo cursed the crow for bring-ing this message, and he turned its feathers from white to black. When Apollo found Coronis and Ischys together, he threw Coronis into a blazing fire—but he managed to save his unborn son Asclepius from the flames.

Apollo took his son to Mount Pelion to live with the wise centaur Chiron. There, Chiron taught Asclepius the arts of music, poetry, history, and astronomy. But his favorite subject was medicine, and Asclepius grew to become a great doctor. Over time, he learned how to bring people back from the dead. Thousands of Greeks went to see Asclepius, for it was believed he could work miracles.

The Olympian gods became angry with Asclepius for helping mortals to avoid death. The Fates complained that their work was meaningless without death. Hades was furious because he had not welcomed a newly dead soul into the Underworld for quite some time. In frustration, Zeus threw a thunderbolt at Asclepius, killing him instantly.

After his death, Asclepius was worshiped as the god of healing and medicine. People from all over Greece flocked to his temples, which were the first hospitals. His most devoted worshipers could be found in the Greek city of Epidaurus.

FAMILY: Father was Apollo; mother was Coronis.

IN ART: Asclepius appears in ancient art, often with his daughter Hygeia, whose name means "health." Several statues of him have been found at Epidaurus. Epidaurus is the site of a fourth-century B.C. sanctuary dedicated to the worship of Asclepius. Asclepius and Hygeia appear on a funerary relief sculpture from Salonika. Another relief sculpture dating from Greece in the fourth-century B.C. now may be seen in the Louvre Museum in Paris, France.

IN LITERATURE: In the *Iliad*, Homer called Asclepius a "blameless physician."

Elizabethan playwright William Shakespeare included Asclepius in his play *Pericles*. In act III scene 2, line 111, the character of Cerimon calls for medical help, saying "Aesculapius guide us!"

IN SCIENCE: *Asclepiads* are a species of plants commonly known as milkweeds. They were believed to have medicinal properties.

MODERN USAGE: Asclepius's emblem was the caduceus, a staff with a snake wrapped around it. A similar staff with two snakes wrapped around it forms part of the symbol of the modern-day medical profession.

Atalanta

Αταλαντη

PRONUNCIATION: at-uh-LAN-tuh
GENDER: Female
CULTURE: Greek
ATTRIBUTES: Swiftness; Hunting

Atalanta was a gifted hunter and the fastest woman who ever lived. She participated in the Calydonian boar hunt, and also joined Jason in his quest for the Golden Fleece. Through trickery, Hippomenes defeated Atalanta in a foot race.

When Atalanta was born, her father Iasus was very disappointed. He had wanted a son. In the middle of the night, Iasus took baby Atalanta to the top of a mountain and left her there to die.

Soon after, a mother bear found Atalanta and took the child to her cave in the forests of Arcadia. Atalanta was raised by the mother bear and grew to be a beautiful woman. She spent her childhood hunting and exploring the forests. She could run as fast as the wind and chase down even the swiftist animals.

Before long, tales of the amazing young Atalanta spread all over Greece. Since the forests of Arcadia were sacred to Artemis,

the goddess of the hunt, Atalanta became one of her most devoted followers.

Will the Hunters Let Atalanta Join the Boar Hunt?

A king named Oeneus lived in a land called Calydon. Unfortunately, the king forgot to honor Artemis in his prayers. The goddess was so angry that she sent a terrifying boar to punish Oeneus and his people. This creature became known as the Calydonian boar. It was as big as an elephant, and had skin so tough that no arrow could pierce it.

Oeneus did not know what to do to protect his kingdom. He announced a reward of great riches and the hide of the boar to whomever could kill it. The best hunters from all over Greece traveled to Calydon to try to kill the boar. When Atalanta learned of this challenge, she picked up her weapons and headed for Calydon.

When she arrived in Calydon, many of the other hunters were not happy to see her. The manly hunters of Greece did not want to hunt with a woman. But then Meleager, the son of King Oeneus, challenged the hunters to race Atalanta. They agreed, for surely a woman could not beat a man in a foot race. But they were wrong. Atalanta won the race easily. Surprised and humiliated, the hunters had no choice but to let Atalanta join them in the hunt.

The hunters set out to track the boar. They were making their way through the forest when the lead hunter cried out that he had

TRUE OR FALSE?

1. Atalanta was the fastest woman alive.
2. Atalanta was raised by a bear.
3. Atalanta was a follower of Athena.
4. Atalanta killed the Calydon Boar.
5. Meleager fell in love with Atalanta.
6. Aphrodite turned Atalanta into a leopard.
7. Atalanta was one of the Argonauts.

on the fireplace was allowed to burn away. To protect her baby, she quickly put the fire out and locked the log away in a chest. However, after he killed her brothers, Meleager's mother took the log and put it back on the fire. As soon as it burned away, Meleager died. Atalanta was sad, but kept the skin and tusks of the Calydonian boar.

Atalanta Gets Three Apples but Loses a Race

Atalanta became famous throughout Greece for her speed and skill as a hunter. Her long-lost father, Iasus, heard about her achievements and decided he might like to have a daughter after all.

Iasus found Atalanta and invited her to live with him. However, he decided that Atalanta should marry. Atalanta, however, was a follower of Artemis and had no interest in men.

To keep from being married, Atalanta tried to trick her father. She told him she would marry any man who could beat her in a running race. Many men raced Atalanta, but no one could beat her.

One day, a young man named Hippomenes offered to race Atalanta. Hippomenes knew that Atalanta was faster than he was and that he would need help from a god if he was going to beat her

spotted the boar. The sight of the enormous beast made even the bravest hunter tremble with fear. The boar lowered its massive head and charged at the band of hunters. When the boar finally thundered away, seven men were left dead.

Atalanta drew arrows from her quiver, and shot one after another. Every arrow bounced off the boar's tough skin without even leaving a scratch. The angry boar then charged at Prince Meleager. When it reached Meleager, the boar raised up on its hind legs. Meleager saw

his chance. He shoved his spear deep into the boar's soft belly.

After killing the Calydonian boar, Meleager offered Atalanta its skin and tusks, for he had fallen in love with her. The other hunters laughed at Meleager, for they thought he was a coward. Meleager became so angry that he took up his spears and killed two of his uncles. Meleager's mother was furious at him for killing her brothers, and decided to take revenge.

When Meleager was a baby, his mother had received a prophecy that her son would die if a log

117

Atalanta (continued)

in a race. Hippomenes went to Aphrodite, the goddess of love, and asked for help. The goddess gave Hippomenes three golden apples. He tucked them into his pocket and set off to race Atalanta.

When the race began, Hippomenes was faster than the other men, but Atalanta easily caught up with him. When she was even with him Hippomenes took one of the three apples and threw it on the ground. Atalanta couldn't believe her eyes. She was so amazed by the beauty of the golden apple that she forgot about the race. She stopped to pick it up, but as she did, Hippomenes sped ahead.

Seeing Hippomenes ahead of her, she starting running with renewed determination. When she drew even with him, he threw the second apple and again, Atalanta stopped to pick it up. In the end, Atalanta gained all three apples, but she fell too far behind to catch Hippomenes. Atalanta lost the race! She had no choice but to marry Hippomenes.

Hippomenes was so happy that he forgot to thank Aphrodite for her help. Aphrodite was angry at the insult. To punish Hippomenes, Aphrodite transformed both him and Atalanta into lions.

Atalanta was also one of the brave Argonauts who accompanied Jason in his quest for the Golden Fleece.

See also Jason; Argonauts; Hippomenes; Meleager.

FAMILY: Father was Iasus; mother was Clymene.

IN ART: Atalanta was usually depicted running by ancient artists. A copy of a third-century B.C. Greek statue of Atalanta is now displayed in the Louvre Museum in Paris, France. The sculptor captured Atalanta in mid stride. The French artist Pierre Lepautre made a similar statue of Atalanta running in 1703. This work can be found in the Jardin de Tuileries outside the Louvre Museum in Paris, France.

French artist Noel Halle painted the race between Atalanta and Hippomenes in the eighteenth century. Meleager is sometimes painted with Atalanta, as in Charles Le Brun's seventeenth-century painting *The Hunt of Meleager and Atalanta.* Peter Paul Rubens produced a painting, *Atalanta and Meleager,* which is on display at the Metropolitan Museum of Art in New York City.

Other aspects of Atalanta's athleticism have found their way into art. One example is a sixth-century B.C. vase found in the State Museum of Berlin, Germany. Atalanta is shown wrestling Peleus.

IN LITERATURE: "Atalanta's Race" is one of the verse tales in William Morris's poem *The Earthly Paradise.* In the following stanza, Hippomenes meets Atalanta:

> But on this day with whom shall he
>   contend?
> A maid stood by him like Diana
>   clad
> When in the woods she lists her
>   bow to bend,
> Too fair for one to look on and be
>   glad,
> Who scarcely yet has thirty
>   summers had,
> If he must still behold her from
>   afar;
> Too fair to let the world live free
>   from war.

In Elizabethan poet William Shakespeare's play *As You Like It,* the character Jacques refers to Atalanta's swiftness. In act III scene 2, lines 155–156, he says,

> You have a nimble wit: I think 'twas
> made of Atalanta's heels.

IN SCIENCE: *Vanessa atalanta* is the name of a red butterfly found throughout Europe, Asia, and North America.

GO TO THE SOURCE: Atalanta's race is in book 10 of the *Metamorphoses* by Ovid.